A GATHERING OF LEAVES

A Gathering of Leaves

Designer Bookbinders International Competition 2022

EDITED BY STUART & LOUISE BROCKMAN

BODLEIAN
LIBRARY
PUBLISHING

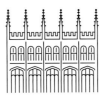

First published in 2022 by the Bodleian Library
Broad Street, Oxford OX1 3BG
www.bodleianshop.co.uk

ISBN 978 1 85124 592 5

This edition © Bodleian Library, University of Oxford, 2022

Photography: Colin Dunn, Scriptura Ltd
Images © Designer Bookbinders, 2022

All rights reserved.

No part of this book may be reproduced, stored in a retrieval system, or transmitted in any form or by any means, electronic, mechanical, photocopying, recording, or otherwise, without the written permission of the Bodleian Library, except for the purpose of research or private study, or criticism or review.

Publisher: Samuel Fanous
Managing Editor: Deborah Susman
Editor: Janet Phillips
Picture Editor: Leanda Shrimpton
Production Editor: Susie Foster
Cover design by Dot Little at the Bodleian Library
Designed and typeset by Lucy Morton of illuminati in Monotype Joanna
Printed in Italy by Graphicom on Magnosatin 170 gsm paper

British Library Catalogue in Publishing Data
A CIP record of this publication is available from the British Library

Contents

Foreword MARK GETTY	xi
Preface RICHARD OVENDEN	xii
Introduction LESTER CAPON	xiii

COMPETITION ENTRIES

First prize	2
Second prize	4
Distinguished winners	7
Oxford University students' choice	21
Bindings on tour	23
Competition entries: the full picture	41
Contact list for entrants	61

EXHIBITION DATES

WESTON LIBRARY, Bodleian Libraries   7 July–11 September 2022

The Weston Library on Broad Street forms part of the Bodleian Libraries at the University of Oxford, the largest university library system in the United Kingdom. It opened to the public in March 2015 following a three-year transformation by WilkinsonEyre architects. The refurbishment turned the 1930s Grade II listed building into both a world-class research library and a new visitor space with exhibition galleries, a lecture theatre and a café and shop.

A Gathering of Leaves will be displayed in the spacious Blackwell Hall on the ground floor. The Bodleian Libraries hold more than 13 million printed items, over 80,000 e-journals and outstanding special collections including rare books and manuscripts, classical papyri, maps, music, art and printed ephemera. Members of the public can explore the collections via the Bodleian's online image portal at digital.bodleian.ox.ac.uk

Broad Street, Oxford OX1 3BG
www.bodleian.ox.ac.uk

SOTHEBY'S, London   21–29 September 2022

Sotheby's is one of the world's largest brokers of fine and decorative art, jewellery and collectibles. Founded in the UK, it has eighty locations in forty countries. Sotheby's was established in 1744 in London by a bookseller. Originally situated in the Strand, Sotheby's moved to its current New Bond Street site in 1917. Sotheby's London offers comprehensive services for clients worldwide. They provide estimates and insurance valuations for all collecting categories and can also advise on shipping, buying and selling with Sotheby's.

   The exhibition will be held in the Kiddell Gallery.

Kiddell Gallery, 34–35 New Bond Street, London W1A 2AA
www.sothebys.com

UNIVERSITY OF EDINBURGH   4 November 2022–25 February 2023

At over 440 years old the University of Edinburgh Library is one of the oldest libraries in Scotland. The Main Library of the University of Edinburgh is its biggest library. Designed by Basil Spence and opened in the 1960s, the Main Library on George Square houses an exhibition space that is used throughout the year to host exhibitions on a wide range of subjects. Designer Bookbinders are delighted to take the International Competition exhibition to Scotland for the first time in its history.

Main Library Gallery, George Square, Edinburgh EH8 9LJ
www.ed.ac.uk

ACKNOWLEDGEMENTS

Designer Bookbinders would like to thank the following sponsors most warmly for their generous support:

Edward Bayntun-Coward
Anthony Davis
Dr Mirjam Foot
Mark Getty
David Nathan-Maister

Bookbindesigns www.bookbindesigns.co.uk
Conservation by Design Limited www.cxdinternational.com
Fine Cut Group Ltd www.finecut.co.uk
Harmatan & Oakridge Leathers 2008 Ltd www.harmatan.co.uk
J Hewit and Son www.hewit.com
FJ Ratchford www.ratchford.co.uk
Sophie Schneideman Rare Books www.ssrbooks.com
Shepherds www.bookbinding.co.uk
Sotheby's www.sotheby.com
Steven Siegel Leather www.siegelleather.com

DESIGNER BOOKBINDERS

Designer Bookbinders is a society devoted to the art and craft of the hand-bound book. The Society was started in 1951 as the Guild of Contemporary Bookbinders. The name changed to Designer Bookbinders in 1968; later, under a newly structured and formal constitution, it became a charity (reg. no. 282081). The object of the Society is to promote the art and craft of hand bookbinding to a wider audience, firstly through exhibitions and publications, and secondly through education. Membership is open to all – professional practitioners, amateurs and book lovers worldwide are welcome. Its annual publication, *The New Bookbinder*, is one of the most respected publications in the world devoted to the art and craft of hand bookbinding. Over the years, the exhibiting members of the Society, the Fellows and Licentiates have exhibited in North America, Japan and venues throughout Europe. The Society runs masterclasses, and a series of practical workshops in venues around the country. The International Competition, in conjunction with the Bodleian Libraries, takes place every four years, although the Covid pandemic delayed the 2021 competition to 2022. The Society's UK annual competition and participation in London Crafts Week encourage new talent to emerge. In recent years, due to Covid, exhibitions have been held online, but the Society, like the rest of the world, is planning a rich timetable of exhibitions in venues around the UK and Europe in the future.

DESIGNER BOOKBINDERS INTERNATIONAL COMPETITION

SIR PAUL GETTY BODLEIAN PRIZES

FIRST PRIZE   £10,000 (binding given to the Bodleian Library)
SECOND PRIZE £6,000   (binding given to the Getty Collection at Wormsley)

DESIGNER BOOKBINDERS DISTINGUISHED AWARDS

Each winner is given a specially designed finishing tool consisting of components from three craftspeople.

The tool itself is fabricated from chrome-plated brass by Bookbindesigns. The handle is a specially turned American black walnut with a solid sterling silver hallmarked ferrule. The tool is housed in a velvet-lined display box with a palladium-tooled leather panel in the lid.

The design is taken from the competition's identifying logo – a leaf. The tool takes this leaf and multiplies it eight times to give a 'Gathering of Leaves'. The design has four leaves which are intaglio, and four as cameo engraved. To our knowledge the combination of both types of engraving on one tool is unique.

OXFORD UNIVERSITY STUDENTS' CHOICE

£500 presented by the Oxford University students. The winner of this category was chosen by the members of the Oxford University Society of Bibliophiles, who met as part of their Michaelmas term events programme at the Weston Library. They viewed the books and voted for their favourite, looking at aspects such as form, function and design.

JUDGES

GLENN BARTLEY   Head of the Royal Bindery, Windsor Castle.
Fellow of Designer Bookbinders.

LESTER CAPON   President and Fellow of Designer Bookbinders.

CHRIS FLETCHER   Keeper of Special Collections at the Bodleian Library.

RACHEL WARD-SALE   Fellow and former President of Designer Bookbinders.

Foreword

MARK GETTY

My father, Sir Paul Getty, began collecting books when he was in his mid-teens. Like many teenagers, he became obsessed by one passion and interest. More time was spent at Warren Howell's store, just off Union Square in San Francisco, than at school. He bought what he could afford and focused on first editions. However, his passion, unlike that of most teenagers, never dimmed and soon expanded well beyond first editions.

The library at Wormsley now includes illuminations, fine print, incunables and manuscripts spanning a thousand years. The heart of it has always been my father's love of binding: from French Renaissance bindings, to English eighteenth- and nineteenth-century bindings, culminating in a wonderful collection of Cobden-Sandersons, and back to the re-emergence of the French as masters of the art/craft in the early to mid-twentieth century with the rich colour and designs of Paul Bonet and Pierre-Lucien Martin. My father was also active in commissioning designer bookbindings, and therefore added the work of living binders to those of the great binders of the past.

Bindings are the vehicles for expressing our wonder at humankind's literary and intellectual achievements and it is with great joy that we at Wormsley, together with the Bodleian Library, do what we can to encourage this great quiet and noble art form.

Preface

RICHARD OVENDEN

The Bodleian Libraries is delighted to present the Designer Bookbinders International Competition, together with the Sir Paul Getty Bookbinding Prize.

This is the fourth time that the Competition has been held, and we continue to be proud to be collaborators with Designer Bookbinders. The strongly international flavour of the first three helped to establish the Competition as a major event in the world of bookbinding, an appeal helped no doubt by the prestigious nature of the Prize. I am happy to say that the range of talent in the 2022 Competition is as compelling as in the previous years, if not more so. To judge by the creativity, inventiveness and sheer technical excellence of these entries, the art and craft of bookbinding is in excellent health.

The Bodleian Library has engaged bookbinders for centuries. For many years publishers would release their works in paper wrappers, leaving the choice of binding to the individual collector. Thousands of titles received by the Bodleian were subsequently bound to the Library's specifications, many still in use today. It is especially satisfying therefore to welcome our friends at Designer Bookbinders to the Library to present this showcase of exceptional talent.

We are enormously grateful to Mark Getty for his continued support of the Sir Paul Getty Bookbinding Prize. The bindings in his father's library at Wormsley are a testament to the genius of his collecting skills. The Prize continues the family's interest in and patronage of the craft of bookbinding.

Introduction

LESTER CAPON

This is the fourth Designer Bookbinders International Competition. Once again it was decided to have a theme, a subject, rather than a set text. This allows so much more scope for the binder and also offers the choice of creating one's own text. The topic decided upon was Botany, a great decision with endless possibilities for exciting and inspiring designs.

This year, of course, everything was delayed by the thing that has affected all our lives – Covid. I wonder how many books were bound in the last year BC (Before Covid), how many bindings had to be laid aside due to illness or how many binders found they had more time to complete their work than they originally thought.

The standard of workmanship and the standard of design were very high, I felt. This is particularly encouraging as the availability of full-time education in bookbinding has been declining for several years now. Of course, many of the entries to the competition are by established professional binders, but for those in the early stages of their career it must be difficult to obtain tuition. We in Designer Bookbinders try to provide as many short courses and lectures as possible, and I am sure it is the same with other institutions and countries.

I have been lucky enough to have been involved with all of these competitions; for the first three as co-curator. This time I was asked to be a judge, so again have had the opportunity to have a really close look at the books. It's such a pleasure to handle the bindings, to experience the differing approaches to the articulation of the hinging of the boards, which are ever more ingenious. There was such a mixture and variety of techniques and ideas: from the traditional to the innovative to the zany! All contribute in their own way to make this a spectacular exhibition. If you can't get to the actual show, the catalogue you are holding illustrates every book in colour.

It was amazing to see all the books laid out together in one of the spacious rooms in the Bodleian Libraries for the judging days. To see them all like that really brought home the fact that each one represented hours of careful work, thought and consideration by the maker. I imagined every binder in their bindery or studio or workroom (whatever they like to call it), bent over their bench, making decisions, striving to get each aspect of the work as good as possible. It was somehow very moving to witness the results of, and the sheer humanity of, all this effort within the community of bookbinding. I would like to thank every entrant for taking the time and trouble to support this venture. I look forward to the next time. Meanwhile, please enjoy what is on offer in this exhibition as well as in this catalogue. It is just not possible to exhibit everything, but all the entries are included here together.

Designer Bookbinders are delighted to be collaborating, once again, with the Bodleian Libraries. They have been with us all the way from our very first time and we could not ask for better colleagues. Our thanks go to Madeline Slaven and the exhibitions team, who have been so helpful and encouraging. Their contribution is very much appreciated. Thank you to the companies and individuals who sponsored the Silver prizes.

Thank you also to the other judges, with whom it was a pleasure to work – Chris Fletcher, Rachel Ward-Sale and Glenn Bartley. A great deal of attention was paid to every book.

Our thanks go especially to Mark Getty, who has taken a great interest in this project and generously given us the means to make this competition, exhibition and publication such a success. He has helped us not only in his own right but also in the name of his father Sir Paul Getty, a generous and knowledgeable patron of bookbinding whom the community of modern bookbinders holds in the highest esteem.

A huge thank you to Stuart and Louise Brockman, who have skilfully channelled all the proceedings through the mists of Covid and have emerged successfully, ensuring that the Designer Bookbinders/Bodleian Libraries International Competition is once again a highlight of the bookbinding calendar.

Sir Paul Getty
Bodleian Prizes

First prize

1 **Angela James** *United Kingdom*
A Gathering of Plants from a Yorkshire Garden, illustrated by Angela James. Osmotherley, 2020/21.
333 × 287 × 33 mm

Covered in grey goatskin with inlaid panels of natural calfskin, airbrushed and printed from etchings. Onlays of dyed calf set into blind lines. Foil tooling. Doublures of natural calf airbrushed lime green. Dyed grey calf onlays set into blind lines. Leather joints. Double silk headbands. Drop-back box lined with lime green suede. The design gives a feeling of a profusion of foliage.

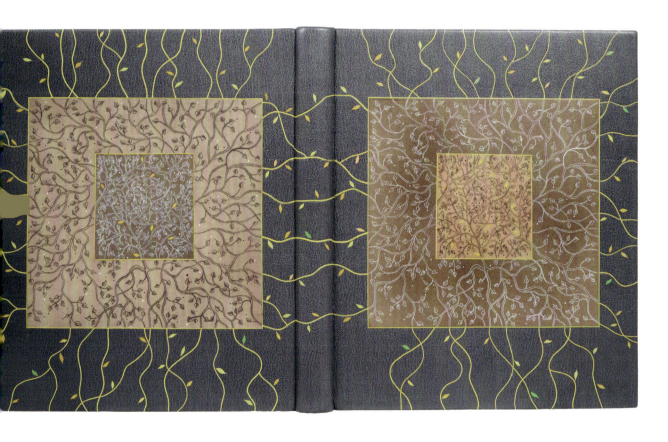

Second prize

2 Tarja Rajakangas *Finland*
Bildatlas öfver Växtriket by Moritz Willkomm, illustrated by Moritz Willkomm.
Söderström Förlag, Helsinki 1893. 304 × 220 × 35 mm

Non-adhesive binding. Chain-stitch sewing with gold and multicoloured silk threads. Green goatskin spine attached to natural coloured limp reindeer vellum boards with linen thread. Blind tooling. The binding celebrates the diversity of nature and the book's hand-coloured drawings, whilst giving them visual space with the restrained design.

Distinguished winners

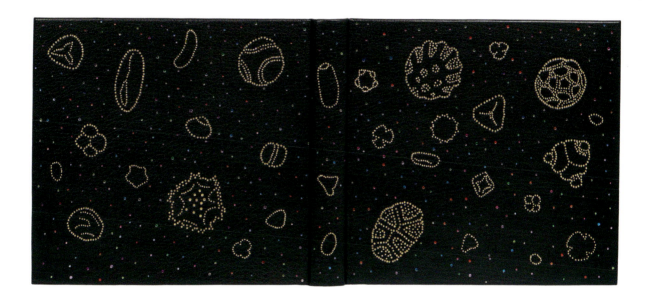

3 Richard Beadsmore *United Kingdom*

Pollen: The Hidden Sexuality of Flowers by Rob Kesseler and Madeline Harley.
Papadakis, Winterbourne, 2014. 206 × 230 × 30 mm

Covered in full black goatskin with matching doublures. Black Satogami endpapers, multicoloured silk endbands. Tooled gold leaf and ten shades of metallic foil. The design is based on the bizarre shapes of pollen grains, with the metallic foil dots echoing the vibrant colouring of the photographs.

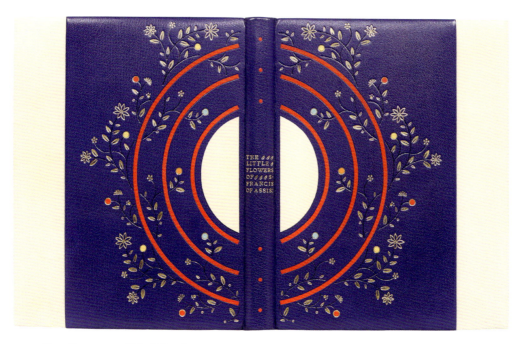

4 TED BENNETT United Kingdom

The Little Flowers of St Francis of Assisi. Florence Press, Chatto & Windus, 1909.
285 × 230 × 35 mm

Purple goatskin with vellum fore-edge. Laced-on boards. Gilt edges. Japanese paper endleaves. Red goatskin and raised vellum onlays. Floral tooling in golf leaf and black inked lines. The design reflects the window from the Basilica of Assisi. The colours and tooling reflect the religious and botanical themes of the text.

5 HANNAH BROWN United Kingdom

The Grasses of Great Britain by Charles Johnson, illustrations by John E. Sowerby. Robert Hardwicke, London, c.1861. 232 × 157 × 51 mm

Bound in full pale yellow leather. Hand-embroidered with species of British grasses spanning the entire cover with stitches added to mimic grass moving in a field. Sewn onto multicoloured stubs and housed in a poplar box with a magnetic closure.

6 Mark Cockram *United Kingdom*

Imbre Flores by Mark Cockram, illustrations by Mark Cockram.
Studio 5 Book Arts, London, 2021. 342 × 195 × 12 mm

Minimalist tight flat back binding. Secondary sewn, full linen/leather – laminated board attachment. Leather jointed endpapers. Full doublures. Hand-dyed fair goatskin spine and board edges. Mixed media, hand graffiti work on paper. Flora appear as delicate shadows.

7 Gabby Cooksey *USA*

Blight by Ralph W. Emerson, photography by Gabby Cooksey.
Springtide Press, Tacoma WA, 2020. 327 × 250 × 21 mm

Blue goatskin leather; brown paper hinges in a Pianel binding with hand-sawn brass cutouts attached with eighty-six flush rivets. Gold foil title. Brown paper pastedown and soft case. The image of roots is taken from the text block, with added layers.

8 INGELA DIERICK *Belgium*

What if you slept… by Samuel Taylor Coleridge, illustrated by Rolf Lock. Düren, 2020. 197 × 107 × 15 mm

Pierced white vellum binding, underlayed with multicoloured Japanese papers. Gold tooling. Visible dyed vellum tapes woven through joint. Handmade paper endleaves. Striped leather drop-back box in half vellum with handwritten title by Rolf Lock.

9 SUE DOGGETT *United Kingdom*

Nine Herbs Charm, written and illustrated by Sue Doggett. London, 2021. 335 × 250 × 35 mm

Three-part binding of embroidered and resist-dyed leather with collaged paper panels inset into sculpted boards. Weeds grow unchecked in the in-between spaces of the city. Ancient plants, linked to magic, folklore and medicine, they thrive, despite our interventions.

10 **Mark Esser** *USA*

Flora Exotica by Gordon DeWolf, illustrated by Jacques Hnizdovsky.
David R. Godine, Boston MA, 1972. 305 × 229 × 16 mm

Tight back, laced-on board binding in full brown goatskin with green goatskin onlays, blind and gold tooling. Edge-to-edge doublures of gold-tooled light green goatskin. Brown suede flyleaves. Sewn silk endbands. All edges gilt. Horse chestnut leaves taken from a Hnizdovsky woodcut.

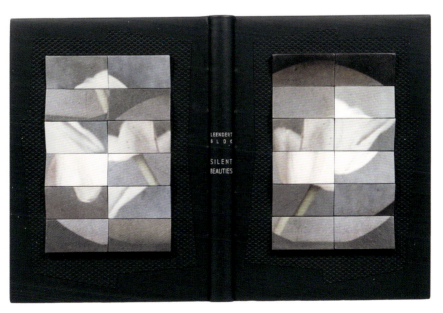

11 **Eduardo Giménez** *Spain*

Silent Beauties: Photographs from the 1920s, photographs by Leendert Blok, text by Gilles Clément.
Hatje Cantz Verlag, Ostfildern, 2015. 267 × 200 × 40 mm

Bound in full black calfskin, embossed black calf onlays with collages in relief of photograph by Leendert Blok, stuck down and burnished onto wooden pieces. Titled in palladium to the spine, hand-sewn silk endbands, embossed black doublures.

12 JENNI GREY United Kingdom

Poisonous Plants by John Nash and W. Dallimore, illustrated by John Nash. Haslewood Books, London, 1927. 305 × 200 × 28 mm

Covered in hand-dyed silk dupion. Handmade craquelure resin cabochons contain leaf skeletons. Metallic seed beads and cordé. Tooled mingei paper doublures. Painted top edge. Walnut box with inset complementary panels. Seed pods harbour a symbol of death.

13 PAUL JOHNSON United Kingdom

Flower Song, 2020, 330 × 270 × 100 mm

Accordion pop-up book. Paper dyed with textile dyes, pen work. Design inspired by the Oxford Botanic Garden. The door on the cover opens to reveal an inner garden. Three gardens are portrayed – the medieval, the Persian and the Chinese.

14 Miranda Kemp *United Kingdom*

Botanical Sketchbooks by Helen and William Bynum. Thames & Hudson, London, 2017.
270 × 200 × 30 mm

Bradel binding. Front and back boards edged in brown goatskin with laminated hand-printed and -tooled paper panels. Orginal etching endpapers with laminated paper doublures. Spine of floating vellum over kraft paper with green leather at head and tail. Design inspired by early sketchbooks of vellum, parchment and artists' materials.

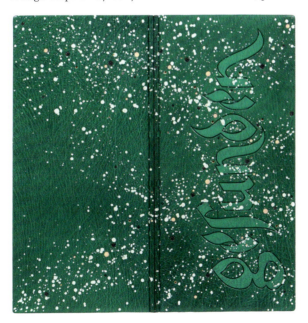

15 Angela Lenhof *Germany*

Gefunden by Johann Wolfgang von Goethe, calligraphy by Margret Grewe. Fürth, 2021.
304 × 148 × 13 mm

Split-spine case binding covered in turquoise Oasis goatskin with woven tape structure. Blind-tooled title with abraded lettering. Specks of acrylic represent a sea of flowers, with stingray-leather inlays, rhinestones and gold-tooled dots.

16 **Anna Linnsen** *The Netherlands*

Schaduwbladeren by Els Kooiman, calligraphy by Bernadette D'Haese.
De Boektiek, Kapellen, 2003. No. 273/600. 315 × 270 × 20 mm.

Goatskin binding with fixed spine, divided into six horizontal parts, pressed patterns of leaf forms. Foiled title. Boards hinged to the sculptured spine on leather straps over metal pins. Pierced boards, spine in different depths and colours of leather.

17 **Kaori Maki** *United Kingdom*

The Abstract Garden by Philip Gross, engravings by Peter Reddick.
The Old Stile Press, Monmouthshire, 2006. 270 × 200 × 20 mm

Covered in Harmatan brown leather; relief printing with linocut and gilding. Hand-printed flyleaves, leather doublures, gilt head. Design inspired by the 'poem-by-way-of-a-preface'.

18 Tom McEwan United Kingdom

A Drunk Man Looks at the Thistle by Hugh MacDiarmid, illustrated by Frans Masereel. Kulgin Duval & Colin H. Hamilton, Falkland, 1969. 292 × 203 × 31 mm

Hand-dyed goatskin binding and doublures with inlayed panels. Gold and pigment foils, carbon and blind tooling. Head decorated with acrylic ink and gold leaf, blind tooled and textured before sewing. Colour and design derived from thistle heads.

 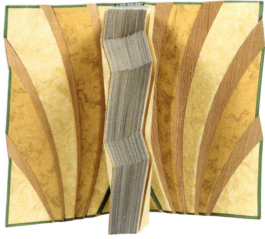

19 Graham Patten USA

Between Earth and Sky: Our Intimate Connections to Trees by Nalini Nadkarni. University of California Press, Berkeley, 2008. 231 × 150 × 50 mm

Leaves folded identically in radiating curves. Sewn on tapes. Covers constructed with alternating curved facets of cherry wood and paper board. Green Harmatan goatskin, cherry spine inlay. Amate bark paper and Mayan Huun paper endleaves. Silk endbands. Graphite edges. Materials and design inspired by tree and leaf forms.

15

20 MIGUEL PEREZ FERNANDEZ *Spain*

Los jardines más bellos de España, Cultural, Madrid, 2004. 325 × 285 × 45 mm

Dorfner-style binding on Keperra and Rivoli paper strips. Goatskin spine; airbrushed polycarbonate boards with several colours of acrylic; leather endbands. Design inspired by a Picasso painting featuring a bouquet of flowers, serving as a decorative motif on both the cover and the box.

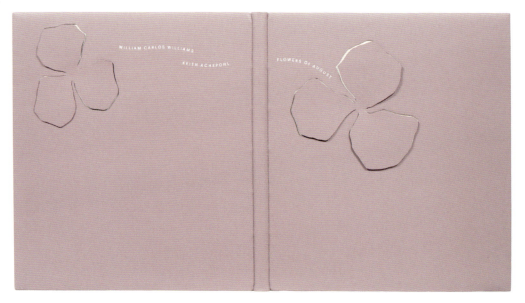

21 SOL RÉBORA *Argentina*

Flowers of August by William Carlos Williams, illustrations by Keith Achepol. Windhover Press, Iowa, 1983. 255 × 230 × 35 mm

Laced-in board structure covered in full violet box calf. Flowers in relief emanating from the surface of the leather, edges of flowers picked out with white lines in relief. Titling creating lines of movement. The inspiration of the design was the transparency of the printed flowers on the paper within the book.

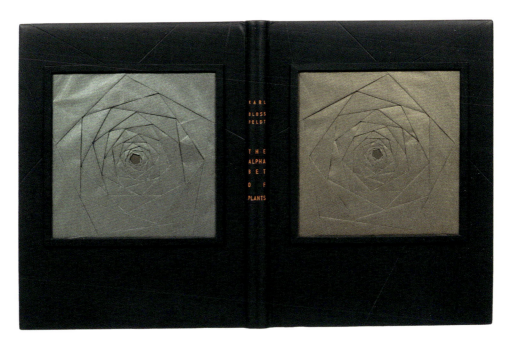

22 ELENA SÁNCHEZ *Spain*

The Alphabet of Plants by Karl Blossfeldt, Neues, New York, 1997. 220 × 170 × 20 mm

Bound in full black calfskin, blind tooled, with one piece of folded paper depicting a camera shutter inset on each board. Lettered in orange on spine. Hand-sewn endbands, textured grey paper endleaves.

23 HAEIN SONG *United Kingdom*

The Botanical City by Hélèna Dove and Harry Adès, botanical illustrations from *Flora Londinensis* by various artists, Hoxton Mini Press, London, 2020. 295 × 194 × 21 mm

Full yellow goatskin binding with sixty-two back-pared onlays in twenty-six colours. Leather joints and doublures. Lino-printed endpaper sections. Hand-sewn silk endbands. Composition featuring the silhouetted forms of forty-three plants from the book.

24 Gillian Stewart *United Kingdom*

The Journey of Thomas the Rhymer, illustrations by Angela Lemaire. The Old Stile Press, Monmouthshire, 2001. 270 × 200 × 15 mm

Bradel structure with hand-dyed green and sunago goatskin spine piece. Boards covered in cyanotype prints with white calf inlays, tooled in genuine variagated gold leaf and foil. Top edge hand-painted. Leather-jointed endpapers with cyanotype flyleaf and paper doublures. Dreamy prints echo the seduction of the faery queen; white stripe of dappled forest light.

25 Daniel Szlachtowski *Poland*

Basilius Besler Florilegium by Klaus Walter Littger, illustrations by Werner Dressendörfer. Taschen, Cologne, 2016. 200 × 150 × 40 mm

Bound in full hand-dyed goatskin. Back-pared leather onlays on covers and spine. Blind, metallic and pigmented foil tooling. Airbrushed and marbled edges and endpapers, with hand-tooled leather endbands. Stored in a marbled, hand-tooled buckram-covered box which unfolds, resembling leaves. Design inspired by old botanical prints.

26 Theresa Wedemeyer *Germany*

I BM G III – Der Sündenfall by Theresa Wedemeyer, illustrated by Theresa Wedemeyer. Münster, 2020. 223 × 165 × 13 mm

Open-joint structure covered in red goatskin, red monotype, gold foil tooling, leather headbands, ivory-coloured edges, leather inlays. 'The Fall of Man, this story of a simple fruit, has shaped gender roles and their evaluation for centuries. But everything can change: we are the gardeners and we hold the future in our hands.'

27 Daniel Wray *United Kingdom*

The Secret Garden by Frances Hodgson Burnett, illustrations by Charles Robinson. William Heinemann, London, 1911. 202 × 167 × 35 mm

Bound in full dark-green cape levant with red and natural onlays; gold tooling. The design is inspired by the text and Sangorski and Sutcliffe bindings of the era. Gilt edges.

Oxford University students' choice

28 Begoña Cabero Diéguez *Spain*

El Jardín del Prado by Eduardo Barba Gómez, illustrations by Juan Luis Castillo.
Editorial Planteta, Barcelona, 2020. 240 × 170 × 35

Flexible non-adhesive binding with raised bands, double cords laced in with linen thread. Arabic headbands, Japanese paper. Incorporating materials of plant origin due to the flexibility of plants and the strength and longevity of trees.

Bindings on tour

29 Kathy Abbott
United Kingdom

The Lyrical Woodlands by Margaret Sackville, illustrated by Lonsdale Ragg, Chiswick Press, London, 1945. 286 × 201 × 11 mm

A simplified binding with chocolate goatskin spine, calfskin vellum boards, Japanese handmade paper endpapers and doublures. Top edge gilt, gold tooling using tools designed by the binder. Inspired by the many references to leaves and gold in the poems, I wanted to evoke sunlight on the edges of falling leaves.

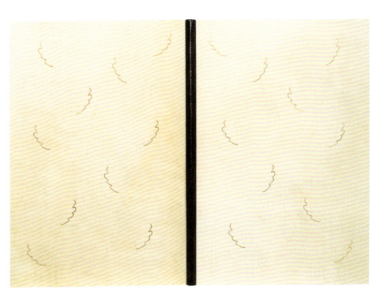

30 Susan Allix
United Kingdom

Acanthus Etc., Pliny, Tradescant, Parkinson, illustrations by Susan Allix, London, 2020. 380 × 290 × 60 mm

Moulded orange goatskin spine, bronze waxed. Glitz endbands. Inset lettering. Vignettes in pencil, acrylic, marbling, copper leaf. Typographic endpaper. Construction a K119 variation using tapes and extra attachment, deckle-edged boards with calfskin and handmade papers.
Non-competitive entry

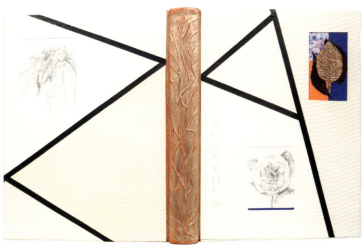

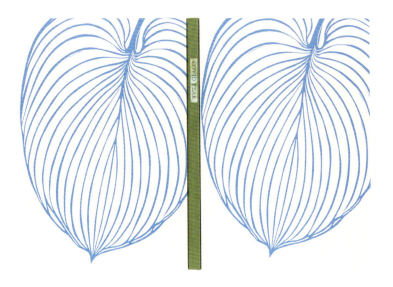

31 ALICE AUSTIN *USA*

COVID Year, written and illustrated by Alice Austin. Alice Austin, Philadelphia, 2021.
273 × 197 × 12 mm

Hugo Peller-style case binding, with green bookcloth spine and handmade cover paper. A presentation of pandemic thoughts and occurrences, with a focus on the seasonal plants from the binder's garden. The edition of ten is printed on Zerkall book paper.

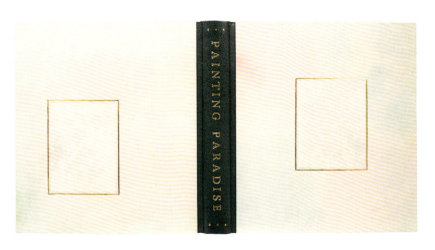

32 GLENN BARTLEY
United Kingdom

Painting Paradise: The Art of the Garden by Vanessa Remington. Royal Collection Trust, London 2015.
300 × 286 × 39 mm

Bound in quarter green goatskin with translucent calf vellum boards. Tongue and slot board attachment. Spine rounded but not backed. Edges gilt. Suede flyleaves and decorative paper doublures. Gold tooling. Pen-and-ink illustrations on cover by Hannah Bartley, applied under the vellum.
Non-competitive entry

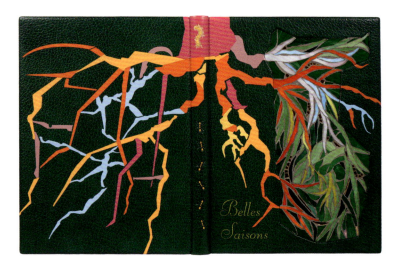

33 FABRIZIO BERTOLOTTI
Italy

Belles Saisons by Colette, Éditions de la Galerie Charpentier, Paris, 1945. No. 168/350.
325 × 253 × 30 mm

Bound in green Cape morocco with Breteuil goatskin inlays. Glass mosaic panel using antique stone mosaic technique gives the effect of a cathedral stained-glass window. Spine decorated with goatskin onlays, graphite edges, vellum headbands.

34 JAMES BROCKMAN
United Kingdom

Under Milk Wood by Dylan Thomas. J.M. Dent, London 1954.
190 × 130 × 23 mm

Covered in full-figured vellum. Cockerell marbled paper endpapers with Japanese paper overcovers. Edges gilt, split boards. Tooled in gold leaf with recessed leather onlays. Original publisher's binding included in box. Terraces of small houses representing Milk Wood tooled in gold beneath with onlays of woodland colours.
Non-competitive entry

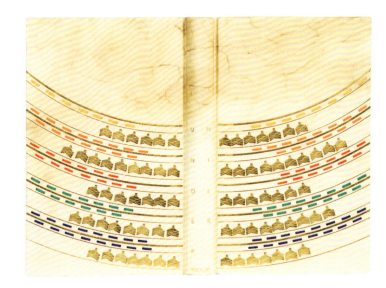

35 STUART BROCKMAN
United Kingdom

Land, poems selected by Eric Williams, wood engravings by Garrick Palmer, The Old Stile Press, Monmouthshire 1996. No. 200/240. 227 × 273 × 17 mm

Full transparent vellum binding over watercolour, gilt edges, Louise Brockman marbled paper endleaves, black goatskin edging to inside of boards, gold tooling and lettering. The design evokes landscapes and sky, including geographical features such as hills and rivers.
Non-competitive entry

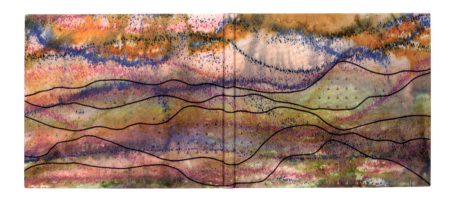

36 FRANÇOISE BUNIAZET
France

Herbier Rhônalpin (Rhônalpin herbarium) by Jean Collion.
211 × 152 × 75 mm

Crossed non-adhesive structure covered in parchment. Brown Japanese paper with clover printing, gold leaf.

37 TRACEY BUSH
United Kingdom

Seven: The Folk Magic of Seven British Wild Plants and Creature, written and illustrated by Tracey Bush. Badger Press, Bishop's Waltham, 2020–21. 225 × 165 × 20 mm

Triple concertina-stitched binding. Pages hand-cut into leaves. Blue cloth boards foiled in black with elder leaf and spider. Screen-printed maru chitsu case, fastened with bone catches, silver-gilt elder beads. Drawings screen-printed onto Canson paper with a sprinkling of silver ink.

38 CINCO ± (Dolores Baldó, Margarita Del Portillo, Isabel García de la Rasilla & Inmaculada Gazapo) *Spain*

Jardines Clásicos de España: Castilla by Xavier de Winthuysen. CIAP, Madrid, 1930. 280 × 210 × 25 mm

Bradel binding with green goatskin spine. Boards covered with painted metal mesh over handmade paper and freeze-dried leaves. Silk hand-sewn endbands, suede endpapers.
Non-competitive entry

39 MARTINE CLAMAGIRAND-ROTH *France*

Litanies de la rose by Remy de Gourmont, illustrations by Andre Domin. Rene Kieffer, Paris, 1919. No. 151/500. 170 × 135 × 18 mm

Bradel binding in zebrano wood, rotating inlaid leather roses. Flyleaves in woodpaper. Handmade striped insects. Housed in a zebrano and sycamore box, with lilac leather strip. The rose, like Eve in the Garden of Eden, is a perpetual symbol of feminity and sensuality.

40 COLEEN CURRY USA

Bokeh: A Little Book of Flowers, poems and engravings by Gaylord Shanilec. Midnight Paper Sales, Saint Paul MN. 2020. 218 × 153 × 19 mm

Multicoloured dyed and manipulated kangaroo leather laced-on binding, edge-to-edge doublures. Gold leaf. Suede flyleaves, silk endbands. Design endeavours to create 'Bokeh: the aesthetic quality of the soft blur produced in the out-of-focus parts of an image produced by a lens.'

41 GAVIN DOVEY USA

The Gehenna Florilegium by Anthony Hecht, woodcuts by Leonard Baskin. Gehenna Press, Rockport ME, 1998, 419 × 295 × 25 mm

Bradel variation split-board Cape binding in dyed and sanded goatskin. Spine hand-lettered in gold leaf. Boards decorated with inlays of wood veneer, dyed and inked goatskin. Black-and-gold hand tooling. Doublures and flyleaves monoprints from cross-section of oak tree. Housed in a suede-lined chemise and slipcase with goatskin and stone veneer. Non-competitive entry

42 SAMUEL FEINSTEIN USA

Le Jardin des supplices by Octave Mirbeau, illustrations by Auguste Rodin. Charpentier et Fasquelle, Paris, 1899. 250 × 175 × 65 mm

Full goatskin binding with gold and carbon tooling and onlays. Top edge gilt and gauffered, endleaves marbled by the binder. The Torture Garden is a critique of colonialism still relevant today, in which the horrific treatment of those exploited within its walls produces the most beautiful flowers.

43 Erin Fletcher USA

Craft of the Dyer: Colour from Plants and Lichens of the Northeast by Karen Diadick Casselman. University of Toronto Press, 1980.

235 × 159 × 27 mm

Embroidered fine binding bound in pale pink buffalo with light grey buffalo-skin doublures embellished with naturally dyed cotton fabric and floss. Handmade paper endleaves with eco-printed inserts. The design displays plants from the gardens of fibre artists working with natural dyes.

44 Gabrielle Fox USA

Winter's Tale, photographs by Neale M. Albert, designed by Kitty Maryatt. Piccolo Press, New York, 2021.

105 × 110 × 100 mm

Binding covered in hydrangea goatskin, onlays of various leathers, gold and blind tooling, magnetic closure. Internal layers of black Japanese moriki kozo handmade, kyoseishi crinkled momi paper, chirimen crêpe and cloth. Gilt head. The binding reflects and celebrates the colours of the images.

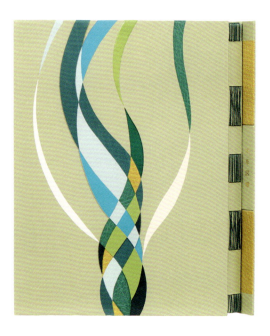

45 Keiko Fuji Japan

Honzō Zufu, written and illustrated by Kanen Iwasaki. Syunyodo-syoten. Tokyo, 1979.

261 × 213 × 24 mm

Bound in mist-green calfskin with exposed spine sewn-on calfskin. Onlaid and inlaid mosaics in green and light blue depicting the images of vegetation. Gold foil stamped title. Hand-decorated kozo washi endpapers.

46 MÓNICA GIL SANVICENTE
Spain

The Book of the Flower by Angus Hyland and Kendra Wilson. Laurence King, London, 2019. 213 × 180 × 28 mm

Bound in full white Harmatan goatskin with six colours of leather onlays forming the petals of a flower. Title on spine in leather onlay, coloured endbands. White goatskin doublures with leather inlays and lilac leather flyleaves.

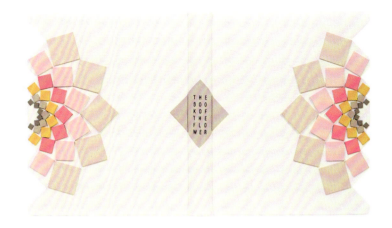

47 WIM GREMMEN
The Netherlands

Disguise, artist's book conceived and illustrated by Wim Gremmen, based on a 1907 song by J.W. Bratten and Jimmy Kennedy. 201 × 201 × 21 mm

Starbook containing flower pop-ups that emerge through a cut-out in the shape of a leaf from the lime tree. Eco prints and paper made of bark, wooden skewers.

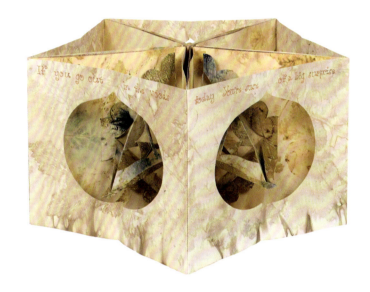

48 YANN GRISET *France*

Plantes des dieux, plantes des démons by Jacques Fleurentin, illustrations by Patrice Vermeille. Les Pharmaciens Bibliophiles, Paris, 2018. 271 × 210 × 23 mm

Binding with wooden boards, electrically burnt design to form Lichtenberg fractals. Dyed fabric spine and guards.

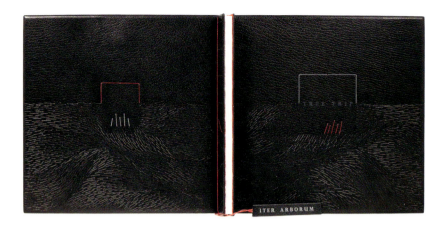

49 KÜLLI GRÜNBACH-SEIN
Estonia

Tree Trip, written and illustrated by Kadi Kurema. Tallinn, 2021. No. 1/2. 270 × 305 × 20 mm

Bound in black goatskin. Blind tooled and hand-stitched with red and grey wax thread. Red washi and grey pastel paper doublures with Kadi Kurema's coloured drypoints. Titling in grey and red on leather pendant attached by red wax thread. The hand-printed book and the binding design are inspired by old herbaria.

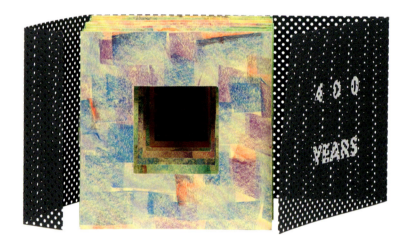

50 LORE HÜBOTTER *Germany*

Gardenkaleidoskope by Lore Hübotter. 140 × 140 × 100 mm

Book constructed with photo cardboard boards painted with wax crayons, decorated with silver mirror foil, photorescent foil and perforated cardboard. The colourfully painted boards represent the wide-ranging colours of the garden. Due to the mirror foil each card shines back vividly, the perforated cover symbolizing the protection of the garden wall.

51 SCOTT KELLAR *USA*

Pilgrim at Tinker Creek, written and illustrated by Annie Dillard. Harper's Magazine Press, New York, 1974. 238 × 167 × 35 mm

Covered in dark green goatskin, coloured and dyed goatskin onlays. Gold-embossed title on spine. Sewn on four-stranded cords, laced-on boards. Marbled endpapers, coloured edges, silk hand-sewn endbands. The design reflects Annie Dillard's observations of the natural world, which communicate beauty, excitement and energy.

52 AMY KITCHERSIDE
United Kingdom

A Gathering of Leaves by Amy Kitcherside. 292 × 246 × 30 mm

Hand-dyed goatskin, with gilt decoration evoking autumn leaves falling and catching the light. Head rough-edge gilt in matching gold leaf. Hand-dyed silk endbands. A series of unique monoprints inspired by local woods are mounted onto stubs and sewn. Endpapers are also monoprints, giving a sense of entering into woods.

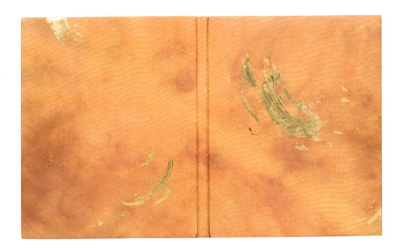

53 JEANETTE KOCH
United Kingdom

Art Forms in Nature: Examples from the Plant World Photographed Direct from Nature by Karl Blossfeldt. Zwemmer, London, 1935. 328 × 252 × 25 mm

Open-joint structure. Vellum-covered boards over a collage of fern imagery. Craquelé alum-tawed goatskin spine and cut-out onlays. Sprinkled edges; multi-green silk endbands. Bark endpapers, handmade paper flyleaves. Embossed green handmade paper doublures.

54 MIDORI KUNIKATA-COCKRAM *United Kingdom*

Winter's Tale, photography by Neale M. Albert, Piccolo Press, New York, 2021. 231 × 231 × 21 mm

Accordion binding covered in black goatskin with multiple coloured circle onlays. Original concertina miniature book cut into single pages, mounted on watercolour paper and backed with Japanese paper. The folding text opens like the blooming of flowers. The thirty-two circles of the cover represent each page or photograph.

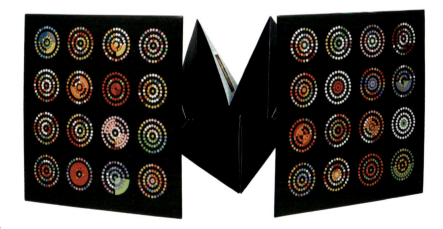

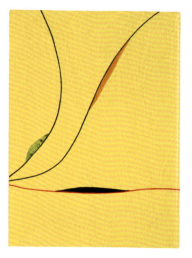

55 Monique Lallier *USA*

Flora's Feast: A Masque of Flowers, written and illustrated by Walter Crane. Cassell, London, 1899.
250 × 190 × 20 mm

Soft, supple binding covered in yellow goatskin attached to the book at the spine. Different coloured onlays. Red suede flyleaves lined with green paper. Design inspired by the flexibility of flowers and leaves in the wind.

56 Malene Maria Lerager *Denmark*

Poetic Herbarium, written and illustrated by Lena Nicolajsen. Copenhagen, 2021.
258 × 164 × 45 mm

Full leather binding, leather onlays. Housed in a clamshell box with hand-coloured lining papers, blind embossed to the spine. Design inspired by the illustrations within the book.

57 Isabel Lifante Pedrola *Spain*

Lorcas Land, poems by Ingo Cesaro. Schierlingspresse, Almería, 2000. No. 17/22, signed. 260 × 195 × 15 mm

Stub binding in box calf with Shin Inbe paper. Hand-painted leather underlay in the shape of the Mediterranean Sea. Coloured foil tooling on spine and doublures. Buffalo leather doublures and flyleaves in different shades of green. Inspired by the Mediterranean flora to which the book pays tribute.

58 Betty Majoor
The Netherlands

Hart van hout (Wooden Heart) by Piet van den Boom, photographs by Jan R. Vonk. De Digitale Drukker, Eindhoven 2021. 205 × 196 × 18 mm

Fritz Wiese/Edgard-style hinge binding. Nepalese lokta reinforced with Tyvek hinges. Wooden boards with ziricote veneer, orange lokta and grey hemp cord inlay. Grey Canson endpapers with orange lokta. Paper and wood used to reflect the contents of the book.

59 Glenn Malkin
United Kingdom

La Nature de Chaumet. Chaumet, Paris, 2016, 318 × 234 × 30 mm

Tessellated impressed leather elements over Nepalese handmade paper with matching doublures. Leather spine with tooled title. Suede endleaves and silk endbands. Edges decorated with acrylic and tooled lines. Presented in a bespoke wooden box. The design reflects the facets of the gems within, which are inspired by natural flora.

60 Isabel Palmero
Valladolid *Spain*

Plantas Extraordinarias by Mario Kuevas. Artist's book, Madrid, 2021. 204 × 209 × 40 mm

Book covered in smooth Italian goatskin. Brown, white, grey and red with incisions and onlays. Leather endbands. White leather doublures. Lettered in two colours to front and back boards.

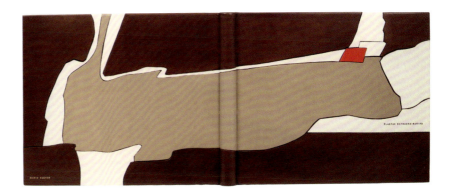

61 Urszula Pietrusewicz *Poland*

The Secret Garden by Frances Hodgson Burnett, illustrated by Charles Robinson. Folio Society, London, 2006. 230 × 170 × 40 mm

Bound in full airbrushed goatskin. Hand-dyed leather onlays. Blind, gold and pigmented foil tooling. Hand-embossed brass onlays. Airbrushed edges and endpapers. Top edge embellished with gold foil. Leather endbands. Housed in a grey and navy cloth dropover box. Inspired by nature's rebirth.

62 Tiina Piisang *Estonia*

Meie mesade seeni (*Mushrooms in Our Forests*) by Pertti Salo, Ulla Salo Kari Puikkonen, Kirjastus Varrak. Printon, Tallinn, 2017. 210 × 170 × 53 mm

Non-adhesive binding with bamboo hinge pins. Hand-coloured red box calf. Coloured endleaves. Frogskin-covered magnetic buttons in the form of mushrooms: readers can change the look of the boards or use part of the design as a bookmark. The patterns of leather reflect the photographs in the book.

63 Francesca Premoli *Italy*

Tree and Leaf – Leaf by Niggle by J.R.R. Tolkien, illustrated by Pauline Baynes, George Allen & Unwin, 1964. 190 × 130 × 15 mm

Full Harmatan leather binding, leather onlays with hand-gilt yellow leather on both book and box. Lettering in gold and black carbon. Three-colour headbands, with gold thread, hand-printed endpapers with self-made linocuts. Binding inspired by the story 'Leaf by Niggle', in which an artist in a society that does not value art devotes himself to painting leaves.

64 James Reid-Cunningham
USA

Alluvial Luck by Trina Peiffer, illustrated by Laurie Schimmoeller. Larkspur Press, Monterey KY, 2017.
243 × 150 × 15 mm

Vellum binding, burned to contrast with images of lush vegetation on the doublures. The design began as a response to wildfires in Australia; as the binding was completed, the binder's daughter's home and farm were burned in a wildfire in the USA.

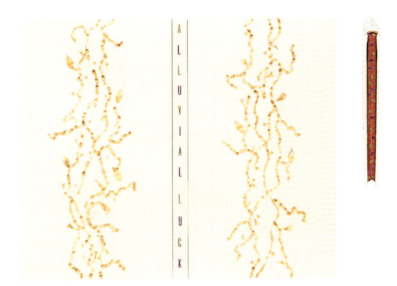

65 Dominic Riley
United Kingdom

Of Gardens by Francis Bacon, engravings by Betty Pennell, Fleece Press, Wakefield, 1993.
300 × 230 × 15 mm

Covered in brown goatskin. Top edge painted. Leather joints and doublures with suede flyleaves. Gold-tooled inlays with painted borders. Gold-tooled dotted lines. Blind tooling. Additional vellum inlays. Title tooled blind on spine. The floral inlays are inspired by William Morris. They suggest garden beds, and the dotted lines the paths between them.

66 Michele Rodda *Singapore*

A Single Leaf by Michele Rodda, illustrations by Michele Rodda. Unique artist's book, 2021.
300 × 260 × 20 mm

This book is a tribute to the diverse vegetation of the tropics. One nature-printed leaf of *Artocarpus elasticus* is used for the cover decoration and content, folded in a modified orihon. The chitsu encloses one nature-printed *Victoria cruziana* leaf. Silver decoration.

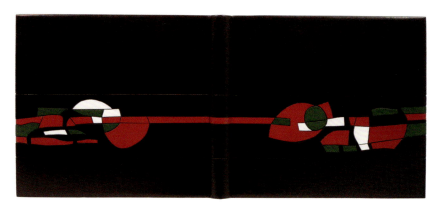

67 Guadalupe Roldán Morales *Spain*

Las Plantas en los Beatos by G. Roldán, illustrations by J.J. Ulzurrun. Artist's book, Madrid, 2021. 215 × 247 × 25 mm

Covered in smooth brown Italian goatskin. Red, green and white leather onlays. Incisions to covering leather coloured brown. Leather endbands. Inspired by the horizontal stripes of the miniatures.

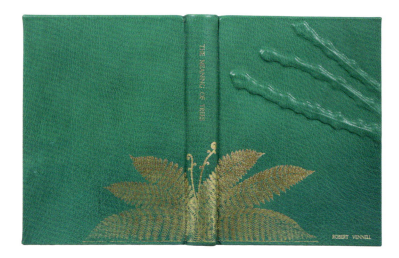

68 Jill Rose *New Zealand*

The Meaning of Trees by Robert Vennell. HarperCollins, Auckland, 2019.
290 × 230 × 55 mm

Covered in emerald green goatskin, blocked with ponga (silver fern) leaves, underlaid with horoeka (lancewood) leaves. Endpapers with cyanotype prints of ponga leaves. Presentation basket woven from harakeke (NZ flax). The binding inspired by traditional use of native plants by indigenous Maori peoples.

69 Tracey Rowledge *United Kingdom*

Sylvæ by Ben Verhoeven and Gaylord Schanilec, woodcuts and wood engravings by Gaylord Schanilec. Midnight Paper Sales, Wisconsin, 2007. No. 8/10.
305 × 212 × 31 mm

Continuous link-stitch binding with the pasteboard covers sewn on as the first and last sections covered with brown Canson Mi-Teintes paper. Spine lined with handmade paper and hand-toned Japanese tissue. Concertina cover made from hand-coloured Saint-Armand paper.

70 George Sargent USA

Peyote: The Divine Cactus by Edward F. Anderson. University of Arizona Press, Tucson, 1980.
235 × 155 × 25 mm

Bound in full blue Harmatan goatskin with multiple coloured goatskin onlays and gold tooling. Printed endpapers with collaged vintage newspaper articles, illustrations and photographs. Design inspired by indigenous Huichol yarn paintings.

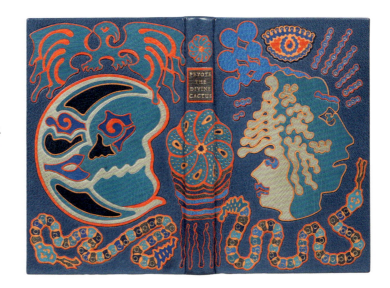

71 Rahel Scheufele Germany

Taschengarten, written and illustrated by Regula Bühler-Schlatter, 2020.
252 × 147 × 13 mm

Full parchment binding with floating back and attached cover boards. Double-sided parchment colouration, interwoven coloured seaweed and cut-outs filled with cyan-coloured hydra. Embossed title. Painted top edge. Design is inspired by tension through the mixture of organic materials: curved leaves meeting linear grasses.

72 Barbara Schmelzer *Australia*

Nature and Other Writings by Ralph Waldo Emerson. Shambhala, Boston MA, 1994.
115 × 85 × 23 mm

Hinged parchment binding in the style of Edgard Claes with dyed parchment doublures. Suedalux and Japanese paper flyleaves. The design reflects Emerson's musings on nature and poetry.

73 Christopher Shaw
United Kingdom

Borrowed Seeds, written and illustrated by Sandy Connors. Whittington Press, Whittington, 2019. 208 × 108 × 12 mm

Covered in full-dyed Harmatan goatskin, design tooled in 22-carat gold leaf. Design was inspired by a fragment of vintage Dutch paper depicting flowers plants and leaves. The endpapers were recreated by J&J Jeffery.

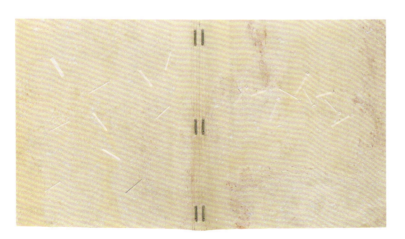

74 Percy So Hong Kong SAR

Dandelion by David Rowland, illustrations by Percy So. 174 × 164 × 80 mm

Staple binding in stone veneer developed by Sün Evrard. Incisions on front and back cover, title tooled in silver. Paper-cut endleaves of dandelion silhouette. The simple incisions and titling are inspired by the motion of dandelions floating in the air.

75 TIIU VIJAR *Estonia*

Karl Blossfeldt: The Complete Published Works, text by Hans Christian Adam. Taschen, Cologne, 2008. 305 × 205 × 35 mm

Coptic binding covered in vegetable-tanned calf leather, leather cord, decorative textile ribbon, Nepalese and Japanese paper. Design applied using batik, laser-cutting, onlays, sections edged with Nepalese paper. Design inspired by the photographs of Blossfeldt: behind every monotone photo there is a colourful plant world.

76 RACHEL WARD-SALE *United Kingdom*

The Abstract Garden by Philip Gross, engravings by Peter Reddick. The Old Stile Press, Monmouthshire, 2006. 265 × 192 × 15 mm

Double-boards construction. Spine of impressed and sanded brown calf, boards impressed and sanded calf with central vellum panel. Wooden triangles attach loose leather strap to the boards. Impressed calf and decorated handmade paper doublures. Coloured top edge; silk double endbands.

Non-competitive entry

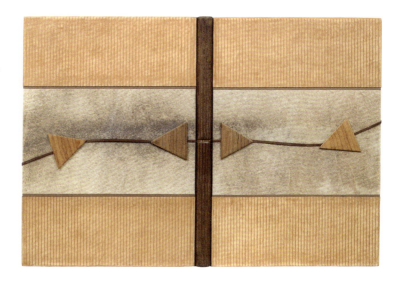

Competition entries: the full picture

Cathy Adelman USA

Ta solitude éblouie/Your Solitude, Dazzled by James Sacré, translated by David Ball, illustrated by Joël Leisk. Al Manar, Neuilly, 2016. No. 5/22.
287 × 218 × 20 mm

Traditional laced-on boards, sewn-on stubs, covered in beige box calf with onlays of blue goatskin and black parchment. Blue box calf doublures and blue suede flyleaves. Design was inspired by the poetry of space and time, the sparsity of the landscape as depicted in the images.

Masako Akagawa Japan

Illustrated Book of Plants for Boys in Original Colour. Tomitaro Makino. 184 × 106 × 26 mm

Full red leather binding with mosaic design in red and green goatskin, gold metal rivets. Four-leaf clover design.

ANETT ARNOLD *Germany*

Poisonous Plants, John Nash and W. Dallimore, illustrated by John Nash. Haslewood Books, London, 1927. 308 × 205 × 15 mm

Dark red goatskin spine titled in silver. Boards covered with specially designed tissue paper.

WENDI BAKKER *Norway*

Still Life – Stillbirth, written and illustrated by Wendi Bakker. Jevnaker, 2021. 325 × 335 × 30 mm

Bound in the fukuro-toji style with wenzhou paper cover, fragile though strong. Flyleaves uncut symbolizing the hiding of information – the birth of seeds and a stillbirth (death and its mysteries). Folded botanical print illustrates the Sufi fountain symbolizing the circle of life.

YOKO BATO *Japan*

Shinra bansho no nakani by Sansei Yamao. Yama to Keikokusha, Tokyo. 2001, 195 × 138 × 28 mm

Bound in different shades of green calfskin with leather inlays, kozo washi flyleaves, hand-sewn endbands. The binding expresses prayers to all things and takes inspiration from the author's poem, writen while farming the fields, about the universe, worship and searching prose.

BRIDGET BAXTER *United Kingdom*

The Illustrated Herbal by Wilfrid Blunt and Sandra Raphael. Frances Lincoln/Weidenfeld & Nicolson, London, 1979. 305 × 220 × 30 mm

Covered in dark green goatskin with pale green goatskin onlays. Bound in the style of K118, so it lies flat when opened. Boards held by vellum flaps. Dark red berries on cover formed by glass paint painted onto glasspaper. Design inspired by an illustration within the book.

Emily Beattie United Kingdom

The Seed Collectors by Scarlett Thomas. Canongate, Edinburgh, 2015; reprinted with author's permission, 2016. 300 × 205 × 70 mm

Byzantine-style binding using reclaimed wood, dyed leather, multilayered resin recesses with natural inclusions and sinamay leaves. Inspired by the dark and tangled nature of the characters in the book, overgrown gardens and poison.

Polly Bird United Kingdom

The Artist and the Garden by Roy Strong. Yale, London, 2000. 290 × 255 × 31 mm

Bound in full red and blue goatskin with green and brown leather onlays. Lettering in gold leaf. The design refers to the waterways in formal gardens.

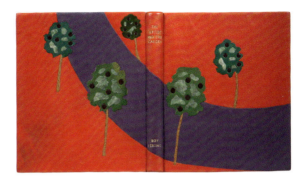

Andreas Bormann Germany

The Baron in the Trees by Italo Calvino. Random House, New York. 1959. 210 × 151 × 32 mm

Simplified binding in shellac-dyed brown calfskin. Recessed onlays in medium brown calfskin and dark brown dyed Himalayan paper. Boards edged with forty-four leather pieces. Lettering, in green, bears the inscription from the main character's commemorative plaque in the family tomb: *Visse sugli alberi · Amò sempre la terra · Salì in cielo.*

Marisol Chávarri Colón de Carvajal Spain

Toponimia de Valsaín by Julio de Toledo Jaúdenes, illustrated by Nicolás Ramirez Moreno. Farinelli, New York, 2017. 267 × 220 × 40 mm

Bound in full sand-coloured buffalo leather. Multicoloured goatskin inlays and onlays, silver foil tooling. Hand-sewn silk endbands. Leather edge-to-edge doublures and vellum flyleaves. Hand tooling in purple and burgundy. Design inspired by the 1784 map by M. Serrano, *Camino nuevo por el Puerto de Guadarrama.*

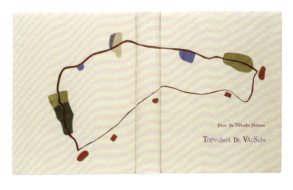

KYLE CLARK *USA*

The Silmarillion by J.R.R. Tolkien. George Allen & Unwin, London, 1977. 233 × 164 × 44 mm

Bound in boards with the spine left unbacked as a tribute to early-modern and medieval European book structures. Sewn-on flexible cords with a linked herringbone pattern. Covered in rust-coloured native goatskin with black and red goat onlays. Handmade paper pastedowns, gold leaf and foil tooling. The design and structure of the binding were inspired by Tolkien's language experiments and love of philology.

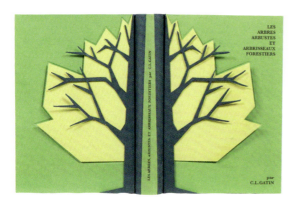

FABIENNE DEVILLARD NICOLAJ *Belgium*

Les Arbres, Arbustes et Arbrisseaux Forestiers, written and illustrated by C.L. Gatin. Paul Lechevalier, Paris, 1913.
163 × 123 × 25 mm

Stub Bradel binding in grey, light green and green Japanese paper. The cover depicts a tree branching out from the spine: the tree is taking hold of the book.

INGEIR DJUVIK *Norway*

Florans konstnärer (*Artists of the Flora*) by Monica Björk. Prisma, Stockholm, 1999. 305 × 225 × 22 mm

Full Harmatan leather binding with multicoloured onlays, some tinted with ink. Bound on four linen tapes with linen thread. Leather joints. Hand-sewn silk endbands, acrylic edge painting. Endpapers by Chris Weimann. Design inspired by Norwegian countryside. Box in dark blue buckram with blind tooling, lined with red suede.

ODETTE DRAPEAU *Canada*

L'Orchidée ou la mangeuse d'ombre by Jean-Loup Philippe, illustrated by Anick Butré. Editions Noir d'ivoire, Paris, 2014. 270 × 190 × 20 mm

Bound in brocade and black tulle, top-stitched in gold thread with glass bead embroidery. Thread, tulle and pink suede doublures.

BIRGIT DRÜCKER Germany

Mein geliebtes Heu (My Beloved Hay) by Jürgen Dahl. Manuscriptum, 2000. 210 × 207 × 10 mm

Leaves bound with coloured threads into a multicoloured concertina. Flyleaves in different colours. Design applied as a collage of layers of different transparent and coloured papers, ink, wax and threads, fixed loosely over the boards. Small white title tooled on spine.

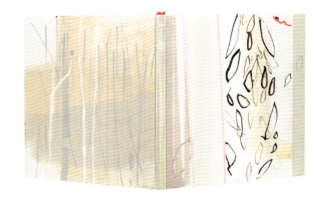

ANDREAS FATOUROS Greece

An Introduction to Botany, in a Series of Familiar Letters by Priscilla Wakefield. Darton & Harvey, London, 1807. 183 × 117 × 22 mm

Painted parchment spine. Boards are a mosiac of dried fruit peels (orange, pomegranate, lemon). Marbled paper endleaves. The peelings form a flower-shaped bricolage indicative of the time before they developed into fruit.

ERICA FINCH Canada

Goblin Market by Christina Rossetti, illustrated by Arthur Rackham. Harrap, London, 1933. 225 × 158 × 75 mm

Full goatskin binding in yellow with black and burgundy goatskin onlays. Papier mâché sculpture attached to front cover. Metal pieces protruding from back cover. Inspired by the Victorian tradition of lavish gift books, luscious fruit from the goblin orchard and urban legends about treats that are dangerous to eat.

PAZ GANCEDO Spain

El País de Lorca by Ingo Cesaro, illustrations by Emilio Sdun. Prensa Cicuta, Almería. 255 × 205 × 15 mm

Covered in full sand-coloured buffalo leather with green leather onlays. Buffalo and suede doublures and flyleaves.

45

James Gardner-Thorpe *United Kingdom*

The Voynich Manuscript, edited by Raymond Clemens, introduced by Deborah Harkness. Beinecke Rare Book & Manuscript Library in association with Yale University Press, 2016. 312 × 235 × 34 mm

Covered in fair chieftain goatskin. Etched and painted steel plate inset. Decorated with gold tooling and pressed dark ivy leaves. The binding design aims to evoke the old age and neglected status of the original manuscript.

Jane Griffiths *United Kingdom*

Natura by Peter Scupham, illustrations by Peter Reddick, Gruffyground Press, Sidcot, 1978. 225 × 134 × 15 mm

Bound in full brown goatskin. Japanese tissue doublures. Onlays of textured and gilded goatskin, calfskin and Japanese tissue. Housed in a cabinet of curiosities with contents inspired by the poems, the materials used in making the book, and the complex relationship between nature and artifice.

Pénélope Guidoni *France*

I Left the Woods by David Thoreau, illustrated by Judith Rothchild. Verdigris, Octon, 2018. 275 × 293 × 17 mm

Leporello stub binding in full box calf, stamped by hand with real tree leaf matrices in acrylic. Metallic wire attachments symbolizing trees. Lettered in palladium to the boards and spine.

Karen Hanmer *USA*

The Family Herbal by Sir John Hill MD. C. Brightly & T. Kinnersley, Bungay, 1812–20. 213 × 142 × 50 mm

Streamlined Bradel binding with Cave paper spine wrapper laced on with binder-made green and brown linen sewing supports. Five-layered boards, Green tissue-rolled endbands. Ruscombe Mill endpapers. Bound in paper due to the appropriateness for a herbal. Colours drawn from the text's fifty-four hand-coloured illustrations.

YUMIKO HARRIS *USA*

The Intruder by Robert Traver, illustrations by Jim Westergard. Deep Wood Press, Mancelona MI, 2012. 254 × 211 × 23 mm

Bound in full green goatskin, fish-skin onlays and inlays. Edge-to-edge doublures in green goatskin, flyleaves in green suede. Blind and gold tooling. Top edge coloured. Hand-sewn silk endbands. Design inspired by the story, in which two fly fishermen's lives intersect deep in the woods.

LARS HEDEGAARD *Denmark*

Norwegian Wood by Haruki Murakami. Kodansha, Tokyo, 1989. 152 × 111 × 20 mm (I) 152 × 111 × 18 mm (II)

Bound with birch bark boards, light brown morocco spines. Blind tooling, top edges painted and gilt. Roma Bütton endleaves, leather endbands.

SUSAN HULME *USA*

The Garden by Vita Sackville-West, illustrations by Broom Lynne. Michael Joseph, London, 1946. No. 332/750, signed by the author.
235 × 156 × 25 mm

Bound in white alum tawed goatskin with pigskin and stingray onlays. Embossed design, tooled with white and pearl foils. Hand-sewn silk endbands. Top edge gilt. The night garden, illuminated by the moon in midsummer, provides a luminous narrative of light and shadow.

TARJA HYVÄRINEN *Finland*

Florabet, original illustrations by Iina Silvian, 2021. 191 × 191 × 10 mm

Acid-free paper and linen-thread *tue mouche* binding. The content of the book demonstrates how words have a life of their own – as do plants. Using the sunlight-exposure technique of cyanotype the design combines photosynthesis and the unexpected nature of the world of plants.

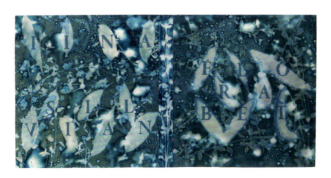

Junko Inoue *Japan*

The Rose by Junko Takano, Atelier Rose & Saty, Hirakata, 2019. 188 × 134 × 19 mm

Covered in full green linen cloth, decorated with embroidered yellow roses and green leaves. Japanese paper endleaves with flowers in gold. Design inspired by this travel report written by Japanese women visiting the rose gardens of England.

Laura Jamieson *United Kingdom*

Pinewoods of the Black Mount by Peter Wormell, illustrations by Christopher Wormell. Dalesman, Skipton, 2003. 235 mm × 180 mm × 14 mm

Full leather binding. Colour and texture of leather created by applying tissue paper and acrylic paint. Hand-decorated endpapers. Hand-sewn silk endbands. Polished edges. Design inspired by the grain of Scots pine wood.

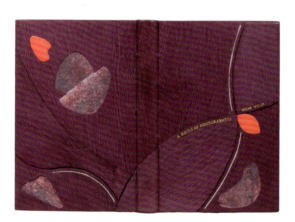

Yuko Kawarai *Japan*

A House of Pomegranates by Ben Kutcher. Dodd, Mead, New York, 1928. 235 × 157 × 27 mm

Bound in full leather with purple and vermilion goatskin. Japanese paper endleaves. Japanese paper inlays and onlays.

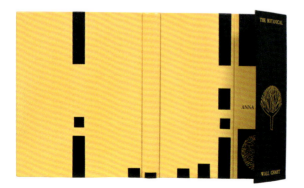

Kadi Kiipus *Estonia*

The Botanical Wall Chart by Anna Laurent. Ilex, London, 2016. 285 × 235 × 30 mm

Full Harmatan goatskin binding, Nepalese paper endleaves. Foil tooling. Onlays and inlays. Leather endbands. Graphite edges. Design inspired by the graphic design and illustrations within.

ALEXIA KOKKINOU *Greece*

Plants, Leaves, Trees, written and illustrated by Alexia Kokkinou. Artist's book, 2021. 342 × 270 × 20 mm

Bound in buffalo skin. Sewn-on meeting guards. Acrylic painted onlays and blind tooling. Double hand-sewn silk endbands. Leather doublures with onlays and suede flyleaves.

IREEN KRANZ *Germany*

Nature by Ralph Waldo Emerson, with decorative initials by Anna Simons. Bremer Presse, Munich, 1924. 281 × 197 × 16 mm

Covered in full beige crushed morocco goatskin. Top edge gilt. Red sewn endbands. Title and decoration tooled with a set of gouges in gold leaf. Stencilled endpapers in lilac and purple.

URSZULA KURTIAK-LEY *Poland*

Books and Gardens, edited by Aleksandra Holownia, pictures by Urszula Kurtiak-Ley, Edward Ley, Edyta Kielianska and Magda Pilaszewicz. Kurtiak & Ley, Koszalin, 2021. 88 numbered copies. 235 × 210 × 20 mm

Covered in full grey calfskin with tooling in white, artistic endleaves. Bees play a significant role in nature. This role is brought to life in a magical spectacle when the book is viewed in conjunction with a smartphone app.

CHRISTIANE LAMON *France*

Fables de mon jardin by Georges Duhamel, illustrated by Marianne Clouzot. Albert Guillot, Paris, 1948. 215 × 180 × 50 mm

Covered in grey goatskin with gold tooling. Brass foliage decoration over black calfskin panels.

Susanna Lemstra *The Netherlands*

Autumn Breezes, by Susanna Lemstra. Artist's book.
165 × 175 × 80 mm

Triptych filled with a poem, incorporating leaves and seeds. Eco prints. 'Like leaves by autumn breezes, we'll be gradually blown away and leave tiny traces of the hidden mysteries in our lives.'

Brian Lieske *USA*

Talking through Trees by Edward Picton-Turbervill, illustrated by Angela Lemaire. The Old Stile Press, Monmouthshire, 2017. 410 × 320 × 60 mm

Covered in green Oasis goatskin, sewn-on linen tapes. Ecoprinted endpapers by Dorothy Yuki. Acrylic board edges. The cover design is inspired by a traditional Cambridge panel and the illustrations in the book. Silk endbands in St John's College colours. Leather doublures and flyleaves refer to the ivy wall in Cambridge.

Cristina Llopart Barastegui *Spain*

El libro de las plantas olvidadas by Aina S Erice. Ariel, Barcelona, 2019. 237 × 150 × 30 mm

Leather-covered boards, exposed woven spine, medieval-style headbands. Lettering sewn through the leather. Dishevelled gold thread on the spine simulates wild growth. The concept of the design is to remind us how natural and precious forgotten plants are.

Ziyaad Lorgat *United Kingdom*

The Botanical Traditions, written and illustrated by Ziyaad Lorgat. 304 × 300 × 26 mm

Simplified/modified Islamic-style binding. Fair calfskin with fine Harmatan goatskin onlays. Gold tooling. Housed in an imitation Wardian box. Bespoke botanical-inspired calligraphy, as was popular in the seventeenth century. Binding structure inspired by a satellite image of the Oxford Botanic Garden, revealing five sides.

Concepcion Luna Sanchez-Alamo *Spain*

El àrbol by John Fowles. Impedimenta, Madrid, 2015. 200 × 150 × 15 mm

Full leather binding over boards in light brown chagrin leather. Leather printed with tree branches and leaves. Orange tooling and lettering. Doublures in the same leather with Japanese paper endleaves. Leather endbands. Housed in box fabricated in wood and printed leather.

Andreas Maroulis *United Kingdom*

The Brother Gardeners by Andrea Wulf. Windmill, London, 2009. 240 × 160 × 40 mm

Full leather laced-on binding, sewn on four linen tapes. Hand-decorated edges. Blue goatskin scarf jointed with grey onlays. Blue leather doublures with leather jointed endpapers. Hand-sewn endbands. Decoration and title tooled in gold leaf. The design represents the trade routes between Great Britain and the colonies for new species of plants in the eighteenth century.

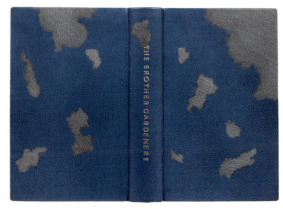

Manise Marston *Canada*

The Second Jungle Book/Le Second Livre de la Jungle by Rudyard Kipling, illustrations by J. Lockwood Kipling. Macmillan, London, 1956/Mercure de France, Paris 1955. 200 × 135 × 50 mm

Dos-à-dos binding covered in full black-and-white calfskin with calf- and goatskin onlays, some hand-painted. Traditional pastepaper boards from blotting paper and wheat starch paste. Non-traditional endbands, hand-marbled coloured endpapers. Gold-tooled titles in English and French – Canada's two languages bound together.

Sofia Mendizabel *Argentina*

Weeds and Wild Flowers by Armida Maria Theresa Colt, illustrations by George Mackley. Two-Horse Press, London, 1965. 300 × 240 × 19 mm

Full leather binding with laced-on boards, in grey calfskin. Decorative technique with incisions, brown and black inlays and reliefs in white and grey box calf. Edge-to-edge doublures and flyleaves in handmade paper. Hand-sewn endbands. Untitled. The design incorporates drawings by the binder of a flower that grows wild in their garden – *capuchina* or nasturtium.

THALEIA MICHELAKI *Greece*

Still Life Leaves, written and illustrated by Georgios Boudalis. 245 × 210 × 30 mm

Non-adhesive paper binding sewn on multiple coloured threads with leaves and buds formed from paper added to the spine. Front cover with raised leaf motif on inside and out, lettered in brown and green foil. Card wrap-around cover with green wire sewing to front.

MING QIU *China*

The Story of Rosina and Other Verses by Austin Dobson, illustrations by Hugh Thompson. Kegan Paul, Trench, Trubner, London, 1895.
187 × 130 × 26 mm

Bound in full dark brown goatskin. Multicoloured onlays. Double multicoloured silk endbands. Green goatskin doublures and green suede flyleaves.

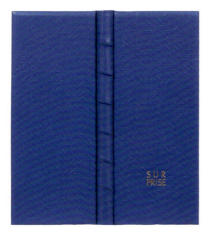

LUCIE MORIN *Canada*

Surprise, extract from *Les Éblouissements* by Anna de Noailles, illustrations by Lucie Moran. Free edition, Québec, 2021. 200 × 100 × 20 mm

Simplified binding in textured blue leather. Diagonal bands to spine. Nylon endbands and Japanese paper endleaves.

EIKO NAKAO *Japan*

A Thousand Varieties of Flowers (Chigusa No Hana) written and illustrated by Bairei Kohno. Bunkyudo, Kyoto, 1891. 185 × 140 × 40 mm

Covered in full navy-blue goatskin, paper endleaves, magnetic closures. Leaves re-edited into valley and mountain folds from the original four Japanese-bound volumes. This results in a book where the illustrations are not split at the centre, making them easier to open and view in their entirety.

KUNIE OGOSHI Japan

Paper-cutting Artist Michiko Yoshida's World of Herbs, illustrated by Michiko Yoshida. Tsubaki shobou, Okayama, 2018. 210 × 190 × 53 mm

Miniature bindings covered in patterned paper and book cloth. Housed in a cloth- and paper-covered book-form box with removable drawers, each containing a book.

MEEN YEA OH South Korea

DMZ Botanic Garden, Korea National Arboretum, Seoul, 2021. 302 × 230 × 30 mm

Stub binding covered in full dark green Oasis goatskin. The book is a herbarium of the Korean Demilitarized Zone. The DMZ map is embossed on the cover, and the roots that could not be collected due to the risk of landmines were drawn using lacquer and gold mica powder.

SYLWESTER PACURA Poland

Seasons of the Year by Simon Syrenius, illustrated by Zbigniew Dolatowski. Society of Bibliophiles/Circle of Typographers, Warsaw, 1975. No. 5/75. 260 × 250 × 45 mm

Stub binding constructed of cotton fibres painted with gouache and acrylic paint. The open areas of the boards are semi-transparent. The skeletal structure of leaves inspired the design.

MODESTA PAKALNYTĖ Lithuania

Вишневый сад (*The Cherry Orchard*) by Anton Chekhov, illustrated by Vladimir Petrovich Panov, Detskaya Literatura, Moscow, 1980.
197 × 132 × 16 mm

Square-back Bradel binding. Bugra paper in marble grey, dark red and green. Handmade marbled paper by Aušra Lazauskienė. Papier mâché cherry leaves. Cherry-tree leaves – becoming colourless and shapeless – represent the cherry orchard, cut down and finally destroyed.

KATARINA PERSSON *Sweden*

Träd (Trees) by David More, illustrated by Alastair Fitter. Norstedts, Stockholm, 1981. 120 × 89 × 21 mm

Full leather binding in dark green Harmatan goatskin with onlays, light green leather endbands. Gold tooling and edge gilding in gold leaf.

ROBERT A. PRIDDLE *Canada*

Herbarium Magiorum, or *A Magican's Herbarium* by R.A. Priddle, Williamstown, ON. 250 × 170 × 75 mm

The style is *wabi sabi*, the beauty of imperfection. The form suggests that the book has had an active life and been taken apart many times, yet the quires are uncut. The paper is new but the materials appear recycled or salvaged. The book is empty but the gatherings suggest structure and content. The book is a meditation of balance – 'As above, so below' – demonstrated in colour and fabric.

PAMELA RICHMOND *United Kingdom*

Roses at Midnight, written and illustrated by Martin Griffiths. Deerhurst, 2021. 210 × 290 × 25 mm

Covered in black goatskin with goatskin doublures. Laced-on board structure. Leather onlays. Tooling in various shades of gold leaf and palladium. Coloured edges. The design was inspired by the artist, who produced the poems and illustrations specifically for this binding: it reflects the relation between humans and gardens.

MARIA CELINA RODRIGUES *Brazil*

Janelas de Sonmos by Lilian Vitral Arbex. Palmarium Edicoes de Arte, São Paulo, 2020. 123 × 113 × 100 mm

Binding covered in white vellum with white handmade paper. Sol Rébora link-in-one structure, rectangular cuts, calligraphic titling on the vellum.

MARTA ROXAS *Spain*

Lettres elémentaires sur la botanique by Jean-Jacques Rousseau, illustrations by Paul Baudier. Marthe Fequet & Pierre Baudier, Paris, 1957. 290 × 260 × 40 mm

Stub binding in full dark green buffalo leather. Multicoloured leather endbands. Gold-tooled decorated goatskin onlays. Textured and coloured inlays. Hand-tooled lettering in light green. Dark green buffalo edge-to-edge doublures and yellow green goatskin flyleaves. Design based on illustrations.

JASMINE RUSSO *Italy*

I fiori nelle diverse lingue (Flowers in Different Languages) by Eva Mameli Calvino, illustrations by Jasmine Russo. Stazione Sperimentale di Floricoltura O. Raimondo, 1940. 220 × 250 × 10 mm

Concertina binding in black bookcloth and decorative paper. Indian handmade recycled paper. Structure chosen to complement an alphabetical list. Inspired by the style of the time in which the book was printed.

IEVA RUSTEIKAITE *Lithuania*

Cartas elementales sobre botánica by Jean-Jacques Rousseau. Abada Editores, Madrid, 2005. 170 × 124 × 15 mm

Dark green goatskin edging, green Hahnemuhle mould-made paper. Tooled with gold foil and green chalk ink. Endpapers of dark green suede and Hahnemuhle mould-made paper. A variation of millimeter binding. Plant decoration inspired by historical gardens.

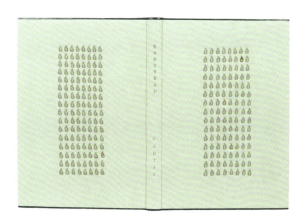

SANGHWA YU *South Korea*

Coexist: Nanjido Naturalized Plant by Na Hyun, 물질과 비물질, 2020. 360 × 280 × 30 mm

Covered in full natural calfskin, gilt lettering. Hanji endpapers. Pressed flowers. The design expresses coexistence by portraying various naturalized plants in Nanjido.

PATRICIA SARGENT *USA*

New and Rare Beautiful-Leaved Plants by James Shirley Hibberd, Bell & Daldy, London, 1876. 255 × 185 × 33 mm

Bound in full Harmatan burnt orange goatskin with edge tooling. Leaf recessed onlays in multiple types and colours of leather with some acrylic accents. Light blue lambskin pastedowns with recessed panel with inserted plant illustrations. Design based on the illustrations within the book.

AMARYLLIS SINIOSSOGLOU *Greece*

The Leaf of the Poplar by Giorgos Seferis, illustrated by Amaryllis Siniossoglou. Artist's book. 103 × 260 × 30 mm

Accordion binding covered in white book cloth, original watercolours on Arches paper, pen drawings on vellum, dried leaves in vellum envelopes, bound as a sculptural book to be presented standing.

DAWN SKINNER *Canada*

Land, poems selected by Eric Williams, woodcuts by Garrick Palmer. The Old Stile Press, Monmouthshire, 1996. 225 × 280 × 15 mm

Bound in full Harmatan green goatskin, onlay of a collage of flower petals and independent petals. Eco-dyed paper endleaves and doublures echoing the flower forms on the outside.

MARIA SOTERIADES *Canada*

An Artist's Garden, written and illustrated by G. Brender à Brandis. The Porcupine's Quill, Erin ON, 2001. 250 × 170 × 45 mm

Bradel binding in red glazed calfskin, red-and-black leather endbands, red moiré silk doublures, red suede flyleaves. Decoration with various polished dry leaves. The real Canadian leaves in the design – from the artist's garden in Stratford, Ontario – reflect the wood engravings within the book.

Priscilla Spitler USA

Garden of Weeds, written and illustrated by Priscilla A. Spitler. Hands on Books, Truth or Consequences NM, 2021. 252 × 160 × 17 mm

Laminate case binding covered in beige Harmatan goatskin; green leather onlay designs decorated with cut-foil stamping, acrylic paint and tooling. Summer monsoon rains in a dry desert town unleash life in the binder's garden, a deluge of weeds, grasses and determined wildflowers.

Geert Stevens Belgium

Black Marigolds by E. Powys Mathers, images by Glenys Cour. The Old Stile Press, Monmouthshire, 2006/7. No. 195/200. 315 × 198 × 22 mm

Boards covered in goatskin, spine covered in goat and snakeskin. Modified binding sewn on meeting guards. Hand-dyed goat- and calfskin onlays, leather endbands, embossed edge-to-edge doublures and sewn flyleaves. Hot foiled title to spine. The design was inspired by the illustrations in the book.

Thomas J. Strasmann Switzerland

Stories from Our Garden, written and illustrated by Thomas J. Strasmann. Zürich, 2021. 330 × 250 × 50 mm

Light blue leather over sculptured boards. Vellum/parchment covers to recessed panels with a variety of decorative techniques. Suede doublures. 'Just as a jacket that is too wide wrinkles around a still-growing body, so the sky-blue leather envelops the 70 pages of this story book.'

Annebet Tannemaat The Netherlands

Bomen mȳn grote liefole (Trees My Big Love). Private Press De Witte Adelaar. No. 52/100. 220 × 230 × 30 mm

French-style fine binding covered in goatskin and hand-coloured calfskin, leather onlays and inlays, leather endleaves. The design is based on a painting by Piet Mondriaan, who in the past resided in the binder's village.

SIGNE TAREMAA Estonia

Yellow, written and illustrated by Signe Taremaa. Pärnu, 2021. 210 × 280 × 35 mm

Bound in full terracotta goatskin, perforated parchment overcover with plant-dyed yarn. The book is a herbarium, with plants lying beneath the thin paper overcovers.

ANDREIA TIBÉRIO DOS SANTOS Portugal

Journal of the Random, written and illustrated by A. Tibério. 199 × 330 × 45 mm

Full leather binding, decorated over natural calf using craquelé technique. Pure gold-leaf gilding and painting. This binding embraces an organic style and is influenced by the binder's location by the sea, in close contact with the sound of the wind and gulls.

ANN TOUT United Kingdom

Garden Reflections by Ann Tout, with watercolour monoprints. 2021. 270 × 170 × 15 mm

Full calfskin binding, transparent vellum, goatskin and paper. Top edge rough gilt, silk headbands, blind tooling. 'Autumn changes my garden. Shimmering light through branches catches translucent drifting petals and enhances brilliantly coloured leaves. The endpapers are reflecting the evening sky.'

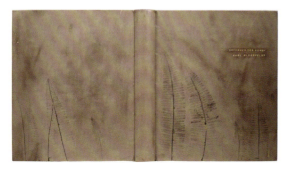

MARCOS VERGARA Spain

Urformen Der Kunst by Karl Blossfeldt. Facsimile edition of 1,000 copies of 1928 portfolio of Verlag Ernst Wasmuth, Berlin. 315 × 290 × 50 mm

Covered in full taupe calfskin. Laced-on boards over single leaves bound together and sewn on to guards. Hand-sewn silk headbands. Doublures in taupe calf and flyleaves in golden suede. Embossed leather with ferns and gold tooling.

INEKE VERGEER-DE BRUIJN *The Netherlands*

The Secret Garden by Frances Hodgson Burnett, illustrated by Charles Robinson. Heinemann, London, 1957. 200 × 140 × 37 mm

Full suede goatskin, dark green goat onlays. Stamped ivy leaves on the top edge, with an acrylic wash. Title foil tooled on leather ribbon. The outside of the book represents an ivy-covered wall; the key hanging on the spine opens the book to reveal a beautiful garden in blossom.

EVA VINCZE *France*

Voyage Botanique, photographs by Paul den Hollander. Paul den Hollander, 1997. 305 × 304 × 34 mm

Full leather binding with laced-on boards. Bound in mint green textured calfskin with onlays in off-white box calf. Hand-painted details, tooling in off-white and palladium. Edge-to-edge doublures in mint calf, and flyleaves in mint suede. Natural edges. Handsewn silk endbands. Inspiration came from the poetic black-and-white photographs of this delicate and fragile herbarium.

FRANCOISE VOGELENZANG *The Netherlands*

A Gathering of Leaves by Francoise Vogelenzang. 104 × 118 × 31 mm

Stub binding covered in Oasis leather. Leaf design to binding. Printed leather doublures depicting leaves.

EMIKO WATANABE *Japan*

A Child's Garden of Verses by R.L. Stevenson, illustrations by Charles Robinson. Mainstream, Edinburgh, 2001. 195 × 130 × 28 mm

Binding covered in full grey goatskin, Mosaic in several types of leather and colouring with acrylic paint. The design depicts the view of the garden from the child's room, showing a window with the flowers and leaves in the garden beyond.

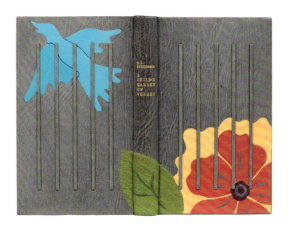

Phil Wilton United Kingdom

The Identification of Trees and Shrubs, written and illustrated by F.K. Makins. Dent, London, 1967. 230 × 170 × 30 mm

Hand-dyed fair calfskin, with reverse-transfer printing and gold tooling, book block sewn on tapes. The colours used represent the range of trees and shrubs throughout the year. The colour theme is continued with the silk endbands, the top-edge decoration and the distressed leather doublures.

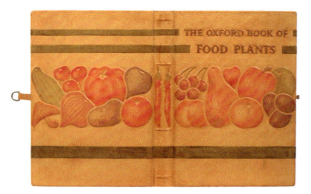

Mira Ylönen Finland

The Oxford Book of Food Plants by S.G. Harrison, G.B. Masefield and Michael Wallis, illustrated by B.E. Nicholson. Oxford University Press, Oxford, 1961. 247 × 180 × 38 mm

Goatskin Coptic binding with double boards. Orange in colour to symbolize the ripeness of fruit and vegetables. Coloured relief title. Images of plants from the book, coloured onlay stripes. Pop-up cut-outs of fruit and vegetables emerge between the hard covers. Inspiration for the design came from the original covers.

Contact list for entrants

ARGENTINA

MENDIZABAL, SOFIA (p. 51)
>   Artruro Capdevila 1236, Castelar, Buenos Aires, 1712
>   E sofitmendizabal@gmail.com

RÉBORA, SOL (p. 16)
>   Monaco 4423, Caba, Buenos Aires, 1407
>   E solrebora@gmail.com

AUSTRALIA

SCHMELZER, BARBARA (p. 37)
>   4/49–51 Mitchell Road, Brookvale, NSW 2100
>   E barbara@barbaraschmelzer.com.au

BELGIUM

DEVILLARD NICOLAJ, FABIENNE (p. 44)
>   rue Louis Hap 17, Brussels, 1040
>   E fab.devillard@gmail.com

DIERICK, INGELA (p. 10)
>   Rue de Spa 51, Plombieres, Liège, 4850
>   E ingeladierick@hotmail.com

STEVENS, GEERT (p. 57)
>   Dikberd 34 unit 9B, Herentals, Antwerp, 2200
>   E info@deboekbinder.be

BRAZIL

RODRIGUES, MARIA CELINA (p. 54)
>   Rua Anibal de Mendonça 32, apt 102, Ipanema, 22410050
>   E mcelinarod@gmail.com

CANADA

DRAPEAU, ODETTE (p. 44)
>   8981 Montesquieu, Anjou, Montreal, Québec, H1J 2C1
>   E odette@odettedrapeau.com

FINCH, ERICA (p. 45)

MARSTON, MANISE (p. 51)

MORIN, LUCIE (p. 52)
>   1402 rue du Parc Champoux, Québec, G1S 1L6
>   Morin.lucie@hotmail.com

PRIDDLE, ROBERT (p. 54)
>   5553 County Road 27, Williamstown, ON, K0C 2J0
>   E robert.priddle@gmail.com

SKINNER, DAWN (p. 56)
>   2895 Phyllis Street, Victoria, BC, V8N 1Y8
>   E Dawn.skinner@telus.net

SOTERIADES, MARIA (p. 56)
>   65, Sherbrooke St East #1705, Montreal, Québec, H2X 1C4
>   E mariasoteriades@gmail.com

CHINA

MING QIU (p. 52)
>   159 Zhengxin Middle Road, Shenjia, Quijiang District, 324000
>   E hghandmade@163.com

DENMARK

HEDEGAARD, LARS (p. 47)
Lindesnæsvej 7, Aarhus N, 8200
E wedderkop@hotmail.com
LERAGER, MALENE MARIA (p. 32)
Klosterstræde 16 kld, Copenhagen K, 1157
E info@colibri-bookbindery.dk

ESTONIA

GRÜNBACH-SEIN, KÜLLI (p. 29)
Raudetee 104, Tallinn, 10919
E kgs@hot.ee
KIIPUS, KADI (p. 48)
E kadi@nlib.ee
PIISANG, TIINA (p. 34)
Vilu tee 16, Tallinn, 11912
E piisangt@hot.ee
TAREMAA, SIGNE (p. 58)
Voolu 8, Tallinn, 16613
E signetaremaa@gmail.com
VIJAR, TIIU (p. 39)

FINLAND

HYVÄRINEN, TARJA (p. 47)
Toini Muonan katu 3 B B 27, Helsinki, 00560
E hyvarinen_tarja@hotmail.com
RAJAKANGAS, TARJA (p. 4)
Sylväänkatu 4 A 7, Sastamala, 38200
E kirjatarja@gmail.com
YLÖNEN, MIRA (p. 60)
Viides linja 14 B 24, Helsinki, 00530
E mira.ylonen@gmail.com

FRANCE

BUNIAZET, FRANÇOISE (p. 25)
15 rue Wagner, Salaise-sur-Sanne, 38150
E fbuniazet@hotmail.com

CLAMAGIRAND-ROTH, MARTINE (p. 26)
    49 rue Gambetta, Rambouillet, 78120
    E m-cr@hotmail.fr

GRISET, YANN (p. 29)
    46 rue Charles Gounod, Roubaix, 59100
    E yann.griset@gmail.com

GUIDONI, PÉNÉLOPE (p. 46)
    243 Chemin de Clémént
    La Crotte sud, le Plan, Vaumeilh, 04200
    E penelopeguidoni@gmail.com

LAMON, CHRISTIANE (p. 49)
    47 rue de Douai, Lille, 59000
    E Christiane.lamon@gmail.com

VINCZE, EVA (p. 59)
    14 rue des Amiraux, Paris, 75018
    E contact@evavincze.com

GERMANY

ARNOLD, ANETT (p. 42)

BORMANN, ANDREAS (p. 43)
    Greifenhagener Strasse 62, Berlin, 10437
    E post@andreas-bormann.net

DRÜCKER, BIRGIT (p. 45)
    Am Wall 75/76, Bremen, 28195
    E buchwerkstatt-bremen@gmx.de

HÜBOTTER, LORE (p. 30)

KRANZ, IREEN (p. 49)
    Ebstorfer Strasse 20, Melbeck, 21406
    E info@ireenkranz.de

LENHOF, ANGELA (p. 13)
    Narzissenstrasse 39, Fuerth, 90768
    E angela@lenhof.com

SCHEUFELE, RAHEL (p. 37)
    Grütstrasse 88, Gossau, ZH 8625, Switzerland
    E R-Scheufele@gmx.de

WEDEMEYER, THERESA (p. 19)
    Antoniusstrasse 8, Emstek, 48149
    E post@buch-objekt.de

GREECE

FATOUROS, ANDREAS (p. 45)
  24 Taygetou str. Ilioupoli, Athens, 16344
   E anrw27@gmail.com
KOKKINOU, ALEXIA (p. 49)
  Roma 3, Athens, 10673
   E kokkinoual@yahoo.gr
MICHELAKI, THALEIA (p. 52)
  Z. Pigis 31, Athens, 10681
   E thaleia.info@gmail.com
SINIOSSOGLOU, AMARYLLIS (p. 56)

HONG KONG SAR

SO, PERCY (p. 38)

ITALY

BERTOLOTTI, FABRIZIO (p. 24)
  via Cavallotti 90, Corteolona PV, 27014
   E bertolotti@marbreur.eu
PREMOLI, FRANCESCA (p. 34)
  Corso del Piazzo 18, Biella BI, 13900
   E rilegatoamano@gmail.com
RUSSO, JASMINE (p. 55)
   E jascarta.rlc@gmail.com

JAPAN

AKAGAWA, MASAKO (p. 41)
BATO, YOKO (p. 42)
  7–37–39 Sakanoue, Kagoshima, 891–0150
   E yoko@batoh-design.com
FUJII, KEIKO (p. 28)
INOUE, JUNKO (p. 48)
KAWARAI, YUKO (p. 48)
NAKAO, EIKO (p. 52)
  3–12–19–501 Tenma kitaku, Osaka, 530–0043
   E Eikomarble@gmail.com
OGOSHI, KUNIE (p. 53)
  1-7-19-901 Higashirurumatsu Kitaku, Okayama-City, 7000921
   E olive101252@gmail.com
WATANABE, EMIKO (p. 59)

LITHUANIA

PAKALNYTÉ, MODESTA (p. 53)
RUSTEIKAITE, IEVA (p. 55)
>Justiniskiu st. 30–31, Vilnius, 05242
>E ieva.rusteikaite@yahoo.com

THE NETHERLANDS

GREMMEN, WIM (p. 29)
>Hoofdstraat 45, Stedum, 9921 PA
>E info@boekbindatelier.nl

LEMSTRA, SUSANNA (p. 50)
>Hoofdstraat 45, Stedum, 9921 PA
>E info@boekbindatelier.nl

LINSSEN, ANNA (p. 14)
>De Thun 69, Herlen, 6419 XE
>E a.linssen@hotmail.com

MAJOOR, BETTY (p. 33)
>Tollenslaan 9, Eindhoven, 5611
>E betty@bettymajoor.nl

TANNEMAAT, ANNEBET (p. 57)
VERGEER-DE BRUIJN, INEKE (p. 59)
>Dirk Hartogstraat 325, Breda, 4812 GE
>E vergeer.ineke57@gmail.com

VOGELENZANG, FRANCOISE (p. 59)

NEW ZEALAND

ROSE, JILL (p. 36)
>191 Mikimiki Road, RD 1 Masterton, 5880
>E spellbound-binding@outlook.com

NORWAY

BAKKER, WENDI (p. 42)
>Prestlia 43, Jevnaker, 3520
>E Wendibakker@gmail.com

DJUVIK, INGEIR (p. 44)
>Gaupestien 9, Stavenger, 4034
>E dingeir@hotmail.com

POLAND

KURTIAK-LEY, URSZULA (p. 49)
    Szczecińska 1, Koszalin, 75-120
    E art@kurtiak-ley.pl
PACURA, SYLWESTER (p. 53)
    Ul. Boczna 1 m. 88, 33–100, Tarnow
    E sylwesterpacura@gmail.com
PIETRUSEWICZ, URSZULA (p. 34)
SZLACHTOWSKI, DANIEL (p. 18)

PORTUGAL

TIBERIO DOS SANTOS, ANDREIA (p. 58)
    Av. Emidio Navarro, 310 A, Cascais, 2750-817
    E atiberiosantos@artenolivro.com

SINGAPORE

RODDA, MICHELE (p. 35)
    The Levelz 07-11, 38 Farrer Road, Singapore, 268836
    E rodda.michele@gmail.com

SOUTH KOREA

OH, MEEN YEA (p. 53)
    803ho–822dong, 70, Jngwan 3-ro, Eunpyeong-gu, Seoul, 03302
    E ohmeenyea@gmail.com
SANGHWA YU (p. 55)

SPAIN

CABERO DIÉGUEZ, BEGOÑA (p. 21)
    Calle Maresme, 248 4° 3ª, Barcelona, 08020
    E charnelabego@gmail.com
CHÁVARRI COLÓN DE CARVAJAL, MARISOL (p. 43)
    Calle Zurbarán 14, 6th left, Madrid, 28010
    E marisolchavarri10@gmail.com
CINCO± (p. 26)
    Gobernador 25, Madrid, 28014
    E info@cincomas.es

GANCEDO, PAZ (p. 45)
>   Paseo de la Castellana 30, 4° Dcha, Madrid, 28046
>   E gancedopaz@gmail.com

GIL SANVICENTE, MÓNICA (p. 29)
>   Calle Pedro Sopena 6-3° Izda, Huesca, 22003
>   E monica@imaginaestudio.com

GIMENÉZ, EDUARDO (p. 11)
>   Escuela Libro, Andador Luis Puntes 6, Local 4, Zaragoza, 50008
>   E egimenez@escuelalibro.es

LIFANTE PEDROLA, ISABEL (p. 32)
>   Calle Villanueva 10, Madrid, 28001
>   E belinlifante@hotmail.com

LLOPART BARASTEGUI, CRISTINA (p. 50)
>   Plaça Dr Pont 7, Cadaqués, Girona, 17488
>   E crisllopart@gmail.com

LUNA SANCHEZ-ALAMO, CONCEPCION (p. 51)
>   Agustin de Foxa 26, 2 C1, Madrid, 28036
>   E connie20554@hotmail.es

PALMERO VALLADOLID, ISABEL (p. 33)
>   Via Lactea, 9-1° 3, Rivas Vaciamadrid, Madrid, 28523
>   E ipalmerovall@gmail.com

PEREZ FERNANDEZ, MIGUEL (p. 16)
>   Rua do Nabal 36, Villestro, Santiago de Compostela, 15896
>   E obradoiroretrincos_stgo@yahoo.es

ROLDÁN MORALES, GUADALUPE (p. 36)
>   Plaza Naranjo de Bulnes, 1–10° B, Rivas Vaciamadrid, Madrid, 28523
>   E guadaluperoldanmorales@gmail.com

ROXAS, MARTA (p. 55)

SÁNCHEZ, ELENA (p. 17)
>   Maestro Estremiana 15 1°, Zaragoza
>   E esanchezmiguel@gmail.com

VERGARA, MARCOS (p. 58)
>   Passaje de los Ancianos 12, Madrid, 28034
>   E marcos.vergara.fernandez@gmail.com

SWEDEN

PERSSON, KATARINA (p. 54)
Gruvlavevagen 6, Smedjebacken, 77791
E k-p@telia.com

SWITZERLAND

STRASMANN, THOMAS J. (p. 57)
Bauherrenstrasse 27, Zurich, 8049
E tjstrasmann@everything-virtual.org

UNITED KINGDOM

ABBOTT, KATHY (p. 23)
ALLIX, SUSAN (p. 23)
19 Almorah Road, London, N1 3ER
E susan@susanallix.com
BARTLEY, GLENN (p. 24)
14 High Street, Culham, OX14 4NB
E glenn.bartley@btinternet.com
BAXTER, BRIDGET (p. 42)
Penn, Upper Guildown Road, Guildford, GU2 4EZ
E baxters@pennbax.com
BEADSMORE, RICHARD (p. 7)
40 Lynton Avenue, West Ealing, London, W13 0EB
E beady.1@virginmedia.com
BEATTIE, EMILY (p. 43)
BENNETT, TED (p. 8)
Longside, 74 High Ridge, Wheatley, Oxford, OX33 1HY
E ebbennett@ymail.com
BIRD, POLLY (p. 43)
BROCKMAN, JAMES (p. 25)
High Ridge, 72 Ladder Hill, Wheatley, OX33 1HY
E jamesrbrockman@aol.com
BROCKMAN, STUART (p. 25)
Willow Cottage, Steventon Hill, Steventon, Abingdon, OX13 6AA
E stubrockman@aol.com
BROWN, HANNAH (p. 8)
Bowlish Grange, Forum Lane, Bowlish, Shepton Mallet, BA4 5JL
E hannah@han-made.net

BUSH, TRACEY (p. 26)
   24 Charlesbury Avenue, Alverstoke, Gosport, PO12 3TG
   E info@traceybush.com

COCKRAM, MARK (p. 9)
   Studio 5, First Floor the Mews, 46–52 Church Road, Barnes, London,
   SW13 0DQ
   E studio5bookarts@aol.co.uk

DOGGETT, SUE (p. 10)
   7 Pembury Road, South Norwood, London, SE25 5UR
   E sue.doggett@virgin.net

GARDNER-THORPE, JAMES (p. 46)
   33 Victoria Road, Sheffield, S10 2DJ
   E jgt@doctors.org.uk

GREY, JENNI (p. 12)

GRIFFITHS, JANE (p. 46)

JAMES, ANGELA (p. 2)
   The Applegarth, School Lane, Osmotherley, DL6 3AF
   E angelajamesbooks@aol.com

JAMIESON, LAURA (p. 48)
   Yarrow House, North Elham, Dereham, NR20 5LD
   E l.jamieson@zen.co.uk

JOHNSON, PAUL (p. 12)
   11 Hill Top Avenue, Cheadle Hulme, SK8 7HN
   E pauljohnson@bookart.co.uk

KEMP, MIRANDA (p. 13)
   20 Munster Road, Teddington, London, TW11 9LL
   E mirandakemp66@gmail.com

KITCHERSIDE, AMY (p. 31)
   26 Woodside, Fortis Green Road, Muswell Hill, London, N10 3NY
   E amykitcherside@gmail.com

KOCH, JEANETTE (p. 31)
   195 Victoria Park Road, London, E9 7JN
   E Jeanettekoch@arnoreinfrank.de

KUNIKATA-COCKRAM, MIDORI (p. 31)

LORGAT, ZIYAAD (p. 50)
   3 Crown Hills Rise, Leicester, LE5 5DG
   E firdoseuk@gmail.com

MCEWAN, TOM (p. 14)
   3 Tofts, Dalry, Ayrshire, KA24 5AS
   E tmcewan@ed-co.net

MAKI, KAORI (p. 33)

54 Hannay House, 23 Scott Avenue, London, SW15 3PD

E kaorijpcom@hotmail.com

MALKIN, GLENN (p. 51)

Woodlands, Football Green, Hornsea, HU18 1RA

E glenn@glennmalkin.com

MAROULIS, ANDREAS (p. 15)

25 Osborne Road, Flat 3, Windsor, SL4 3EG

E andmaroulis@gmail.com

RICHMOND, PAMELA (p. 54)

9 The Green, Bishops Norton, Gloucester, GL2 9LP

E pamelarichmondbookbinder@gmail.com

RILEY, DOMINIC (p. 35)

13 Blake Lane, Sandiway, Northwich, CW8 2NW

E dominicbookbinder@gmail.com

ROWLEDGE, TRACEY (p. 36)

SHAW, CHRISTOPHER (p. 38)

1 Kennel Cottages, Cottisford, Brackley, NN13 5SS

E christopher-shaw1@hotmail.co.uk

SONG, HAEIN (p. 17)

8 Monro Way, Hackney, London, E5 8NZ

E songhaein@gmail.com

STEWART, GILLIAN (p. 18)

Juju Books, Rogart St Campus, 4 Rogart St, Glasgow, G40 2AA

E gilliancstewart@gmail.com

TOUT, ANN (p. 58)

WARD-SALE, RACHEL (p. 39)

Star Brewery, Castle Ditch Lane, Lewes, BN7 1YJ

E rachel@bookbindersoflewes.co.uk

WILTON, PHIL (p. 60)

22 Chene Road, Wimborne, BH21 2AH

E pmw111@hotmail.co.uk

WRAY, DANIEL (p. 19)

97 Wickham Road, Brockley, London, SE4 1NH

E danwray100@gmail.com

UNITED STATES OF AMERICA

ADELMAN, CATHY (p. 41)
1162 Penland Road #156, Penland, NC 28765
E cathyadelman@gmail.com

AUSTIN, ALICE (p. 24)
1024 Carpenter Street, Philadelphia, PA 19147
E amaustin@mac.com

CLARK, KYLE (p. 44)
8083 Fieldcrest Drive, Brighton, MI 48116
E kyle.anthony.clark@gmail.com

COOKSEY, GABBY (p. 9)
5657 S Thompson Avenue, Tacoma, WA 98408
E boundbycooksey@aol.com

CURRY, COLEEN (p. 27)
280 Pacific Way, Muir Beach, CA 94965
E coleen.curry@gmail.com

DOVEY, GAVIN (p. 27)
6 West Lanes, Pound Ridge, NY 10576
E info@paperdragonbooks.com

ESSER, MARK (p. 11)
555 South Water Street #318, Providence, RI 02903
E messer33@gmail.com

FEINSTEIN, SAMUEL (p. 27)
3300 W Wrightwood Avenue, Apt Gdn, Chicago, IL 60647
E samuelbfeinstein@yahoo.com

FLETCHER, ERIN (p. 28)

FOX, GABRIELLE (p. 28)
3673 Stettinius Avenue, Cincinnati, OH 45208
E fox4book@gmail.com

HANMER, KAREN (p. 46)
709 Rosedale Road, Glenview, IL 60025
E karen@karenhanmer.com

HARRIS, YUMIKO (p. 47)

HULME, SUSAN (p. 47)
5020 Hulme Lane, Franklin, TN 37064
E susan@susanhulmebooks.com

KELLAR, SCOTT (p. 30)

LALLIER, MONIQUE (p. 32)
1098 Freemason Drive, Greensboro, NC 27407
E moniquelallier87@gmail.com

LIESKE, BRIAN (p. 50)
       616 Hayes Street, San Francisco, CA 94102
       E usagibrian@juno.com

PATTEN, GRAHAM (p. 15)

REID-CUNNINGHAM, JAMES (p. 35)
       10 Harrington Road, Cambridge, MA 02140
       E james@reid-cunningham.com

SARGENT, GEORGE (p. 37)
       670 Park Avenue, Woonsocket, RI 02895
       E dragonflybindery@gmail.com

SARGENT, PATRICIA (p. 56)
       670 Park Avenue, Woonsocket, RI 02895
       E dragonflybindery@gmail.com

SPITLER, PRISCILLA (p. 57)
       404 N Cedar Street, Truth or Consequences, NM 87901
       E prispit@gmail.com